PARTNERS IN LIFE AND WORK

Providing candid advice on the ups and downs of entrepreneurship, this book interweaves the world of tech start-ups, the American immigrant experience, and the realities of running a business with your life partner.

Across two decades as entrepreneurs, Elma and Dov Levy faced economic recessions, government shutdowns, work–life balance issues, leadership conflicts, and the emotions of letting go of their company Dovel Technologies – a technology consulting firm that they grew from a space in their attic to a multimillion-dollar operation with major government contracts. In this conversational and practical book they share insights on:

- How next-generation entrepreneurs can develop business relationships and networking skills, and maintain a high level of risk tolerance and manage risks strategically, including how and when to scale the business.
- How to stay true to guiding principles as co-owner spouses and woman-owned business entrepreneurs.
- What trends and opportunities to watch out for in a post-COVID-19 world.

Aspiring entrepreneurs, growth-focused founders, family business owners, and government and technology professionals will especially value the Levys' business and personal success stories, with guidance on how to manage a marriage and business simultaneously, creating boundaries with a home office, and showing mutual respect in the boardroom.

T0320969

Elma Levy is an entrepreneur, investor, leadership coach, and public speaker. She is cofounder and principal (with her husband, Dov) of the Eldov Group, LLC, a boutique investment and start-up advisory in the Washington, D.C., area. As an advisor to entrepreneurs, Ms. Levy provides advice on corporate governance, financial management, and tactical planning. In 2000, she cofounded Dovel Technologies, building and supporting information technology (IT) systems for the U.S. government. Over the next 18 years, she served as chief executive officer and later as chair of the board, overseeing corporate governance and managing the company's infrastructure development and growth through its 2019 acquisition. She is also a credentialed leadership, wellness, and life skills coach, and founder of Coach To Strength LLC.

Dov Levy is an entrepreneur, investor, and a leading expert in large-scale mission-critical IT solutions. He cofounded Dovel Technologies and served as its chief technologist until the company's acquisition in 2019, remaining a dynamic leader at the forefront of technological innovations. Over the past three decades, Mr. Levy served in technology leadership positions for the U.S. government's most significant mission-critical projects, including systems for the U.S. Securities and Exchange Commission (SEC) and the Department of Defense (DoD). He is cofounder and principal (with his wife, Elma) of the Eldov Group, LLC, and a senior advisor for GrantSolutions.gov, managing a large-scale implementation of cloud computing, event sourcing, machine learning, blockchain, and artificial intelligence.

PARTNERS IN LIFE AND WORK

Finding Success Through a Partner Business

Elma Levy and Dov Levy

Routledge
Taylor & Francis Group

NEW YORK AND LONDON

Cover image: photograph taken by Eleanor Kaufman (authors own rights to image)

First published 2023
by Routledge
605 Third Avenue, New York, NY 10158

and by Routledge
4 Park Square, Milton Park, Abingdon, Oxon, OX14 4RN

Routledge is an imprint of the Taylor & Francis Group, an informa business

Library of Congress Cataloging-in-Publication Data
Names: Levy, Elma, author. | Levy, Dov, author.
Title: Partners in life and work : finding success through a partner
  business / Elma Levy and Dov Levy.
Description: New York, NY : Routledge, 2022. | Includes bibliographical
  references and index.
Identifiers: LCCN 2022002659 | ISBN 9781032197463 (hbk) |
  ISBN 9781032197289 (pbk) | ISBN 9781003260653 (ebk)
Subjects: LCSH: Entrepreneurship. | Businesspeople. | Success in business.
  | Work-life balance.
Classification: LCC HB615 .L485 2022 | DDC 658.4/21—dc23/eng/20220404
LC record available at https://lccn.loc.gov/2022002659

ISBN: 978-1-032-19746-3 (hbk)
ISBN: 978-1-032-19728-9 (pbk)
ISBN: 978-1-003-26065-3 (ebk)

DOI: 10.4324/9781003260653

Typeset in Sabon
by Apex CoVantage, LLC

Dor Le Dor (Hebrew: Generation to Generation)

This book is dedicated to

Our parents:
>David Levy & Amitza Levy Bruchstein, Givat Shapira, Israel
>>You dreamed that Dov would study in America; if only you could see him now.

>Piet Jong & Alida Jong-Van Velzen, Blokker, The Netherlands
>>Despite not understanding why Elma left, you proudly supported her.

Our children:
>Mark Daniel Levy, McLean, Virginia
>Karyn Alida Krutilla, Bothell, Washington State
>>More than anything, you are our pride and joy.

Our granddaughter:
>Isabelle Marie Krutilla
>>Read and understand your family heritage and legacy.

Our future generations:
>May you find your way to bring value to the world.

CONTENTS

INTRODUCTION

*Partners in Life and Work: Finding Success
Through a Partner Business*

Dear Reader,

You picked up this book, and you are leafing through it to see if it holds anything of value for you. As the authors, we, Dov and I, hope you will because that is the main objective behind writing this book and sharing our story.

This story is about a partnership, business, marriage, about everything we experienced and learned, about the luck and the challenges, and about the people we met. Along the way, we developed resilience and perseverance and trust in ourselves and each other; we learned to tolerate and manage risk and to "take on" and let go; we recognized our strengths and weaknesses, and, as a result, we learned that our success was possible only because of our **Partnership in Life and Work.**

To be honest, as we were living our lives together over the last four decades, we didn't think we were doing anything unusual, definitely not something to "write about". We were busy working, raising our family, and building a business, putting one foot in front of the other and one stone on top of the other until one day, we looked back and realized that we created a unique story of immigrants, entrepreneurs, marriage, and partnership; we recognized that all the, seemingly unrelated, experiences came together like pieces of a puzzle for which we did not have an example at the start of the journey. "And then it all came together".

We frequently do not realize that everything we do, every challenge, every success, and failure, every adventure and risk, and every life change, create a tapestry of experiences that becomes "your story" and that the story could only be possible because of all the different pieces. This is what happened with us, and with that recognition came the thought that we had something to share that could be of value to others.

When friends and family began urging us to write a book and share our experiences, we recognized that what we learned along the way could be useful to those who travel a similar path. **Couples** frequently ask us for advice about combining marriage and business, something we talk about in our book. **Entrepreneurs** want to hear how we got started and what our recipe for success is (hint: every path is different). **Immigrants** like to read about the successful experiences of fellow immigrants. **Business owners** who experience the typical organizational life-cycle challenges of a growing company may find comfort in learning that their experience is not unique and perhaps find a few nuggets of wisdom that might work for them. **Women business owners** who may ask themselves if their experience is unique (hint: it is not).

Finally, this book is for our children, and for our children's children so that they learn the history of their legacy, and for our friends and families, some of whom traveled part of the way with us and others who have known us from the very beginning.

We hope that you enjoy reading our story and that you find value in our experiences. Good luck with your journey, and don't forget to step back occasionally to admire your own story.

Elma and Dov

ACKNOWLEDGMENTS

Where to even begin recognizing and acknowledging those whom we've crossed paths with and who have made an impact on our lives. We hope we make you proud!

Thank you, Mark and Karyn.

For hanging in there with us. It is not easy to be the children of immigrants who are entrepreneurs; the many hours we had to put in to build our company came at a cost to us as a family. We raised you to be strong, independent, value-adding citizens. We are so proud to see the adults you have become; we love you more than words can tell! We hope you will enjoy this book and pass it on to your children and your children's children.

Thank you, Robert and Susan Fratkin.

For inviting us to stay in your basement for 15 months when we first arrived in the U.S., with no funds to go anyplace else. You helped us get on our feet, supported us in getting married, and without your help, we would never have made it through the first 1.5 years.

Thank you, Dr. Thomas Woteki (aka Dr. Who)

For giving Dov this first job after graduating with his MSc. It enabled us to rent an apartment and put a payment on a small car (a bright red Nissan Pulsar). Prior to that first paycheck, our total net worth was around $100, and you gave us the opportunity to climb up! In addition, you and your business partners, Alan and Ed, offered junior partnership status to Dov. Unfortunately, the company did not survive, but we will never forget your confidence in Dov.

It was also Dr. Who who, years later, called Dov when he needed a technical architect for a contract at BDM, Inc to the SEC, called EDGAR. This is what started Dov's career with information technology government contracting.

Thank you, Bill McQuiggan.

For working with Dov, as a Program Manager to EDGAR, and as a role model and mentor. Bill also honored us by serving as Elma's business mentor during the start-up phase, and later, as CEO of our company. Bill's involvement with us during the start-up phase made people notice us because of his reputation in the government contracting industry.

Thank you, IDC Team (Integrated Data Corporation): Greg, Elliot, Les, Nancy, Denise, Linda, and many more.

For believing in us when "the company" was just two people working out of their attic and when our corporate domain name was IDC.TV! It takes a lot of confidence and trust to join a start-up; you worked hard and shared in the pride of our first real office space (Tysons Corner), first prime contract (the Food and Drug Administration), and overall scaling and maturing. You experienced the challenges and obstacles, as well as the thrills and excitement, that come with the early phases of an organizational life cycle. When we decided that we needed to move from shared office space to our own space and change our name, you were the ones selecting the Dovel name. It became a major name until the last transaction in 2021

Thank you, Dovel Team: too many to mention, but you know who you are

For providing the quality services and technical expertise for which Dovel became known, for your loyalty, integrity, energy, and efforts. Without you, the Dovel story could never have become a success story. Over the years, many of you have come and gone, and we remember most of you. We hope that your time at Dovel has added value to your career and that you look back with gratitude; we certainly remember you with gratitude.

Thank you, Paul Leslie.

For believing in us as a team, for seeing the potential in Dovel, for recognizing the need for a shift in strategy, and for your leadership during the chapters leading up to our exit. Your reputation for integrity and confidence is well deserved.

Thank you, Linda Berdine.

For your guidance, support, and friendship and for sharing your experience and knowledge.

Thank you, Jeffrey Gutman.

We would be totally amiss if we didn't recognize the considerable efforts of our dear friend Jeff. When we asked him if he would be open to reviewing a draft of this book, we didn't know how much time and energy he would give to it and how precious his thoughtful feedback and comments were to us. Jeff, we recognize your input and thank you for your friendship, dedication, and valuable feedback. This book is better as a result of your reviews and suggestions.

Part I

PROLOGUE

1

THE DOV AND ELMA STORY

Dov and Elma come from completely different parts of the world, with very different cultures, but somehow, they've managed to build a beautiful life together.

"We built the American dream, as a first-generation immigrant family with two children, our own house, American college educations, and a business that grew from 2 people to 2,500 at the time of final sale in October 2021. We're both U.S. citizens, and we're 'all in'".

From a romance that began on the beach of Israel in 1979 to their lives together as business partners, this is a story of a farmer's daughter from a small village in the Netherlands, who helped her parents in the tulip fields and aspired to a more adventurous path in life, and an enterprising young military officer from a moshav in Israel who earned an undergraduate degree Tel Aviv and a graduate degree in computer science in Washington D.C.

"We believe that our cross-cultural backgrounds contributed to our success as entrepreneurs through perseverance, resilience, risk tolerance, and yes, a bit of luck".

Intrigued? Just keep reading. . .

DOI: 10.4324/9781003260653-2

Dov Before Elma

I grew up in a moshav (small communal village) in Israel, with 33 families. My mother was a homemaker, and my father worked in Egged – the Israeli bus company. We had lots of space to roam around and do anything that came into our minds. I came back from school, did my homework as quickly as possible, went outside to play until I heard my mother calling for dinner. At that stage of my life, I learned how to tinker with things. For example, I built a telephone between my house and that of my best friend who lived across the park of the moshav, involving high-voltage lines going between the trees in the village. Despite some teenage troublemaking, I managed to complete high school and complete my mandatory army service, including an additional year as an officer in the Israeli Tank Force, where I spent most of my time in the Golan Heights and the Sinai desert. Because of my father's relentless insistence that I attend university, I enrolled at Tel Aviv University at age 21 to study geodetic science; even though I had no idea what geodetic science entailed, it was an excellent way to get my father off my back. So, in 1978 I, together with a friend, whom I had met in the army and with whom I have a very close friendship until today, began studying geodetic science at Tel Aviv University.

We soon learned that this line of work involved surveying outdoors, a scorching and unpleasant experience, even back in the 1970s. We also got introduced to computers because of the large amount of data-processing requirements for our projects, and soon we realized that our interest was really in computer science, not just because of the cooler work environment (a vital point, nevertheless) but also because it was new and significantly more interesting. So, we researched switching our major to computer science, which, in those years, at Tel Aviv University wasn't trivial. It involved taking multiple extra classes and a lot of spare time that we didn't have. One day someone gave us a thought of completing our bachelor's degree at Tel Aviv University and attending graduate school in the U.S. "Great idea . . . we're doing this", we both said.

Elma and I met sometime during my student years when she and two of her friends from The Netherlands came to visit my friends in Israel for two weeks in the summer of 1979. We had a wonderful summer romance, after which I sent her one letter and put her out of my mind. That is, until September 1980, when she and her friends returned and stayed for a year to work in a kibbutz and later in a hospital as they were registered nurses. We began dating again almost immediately upon her return, and we have been together until today.

I shared with her my plan to study for my master's in computer science in the U.S. and was so determined that, when my friend's circumstances changed and he no longer was able to go through with it, I said, "This is the plan, and am going to accomplish it!"

Elma Before Dov

There are times in your life when you know that everything will be different from that moment on; most everyone has moments like that. My "moment" was seemingly insignificant, but looking back, it was the "aha" moment that determined my direction.

I grew up the second girl in a Catholic family of four; Mom was a homemaker, and Dad was a farmer. We harvested vegetables during most of the year and tulip bulbs in the summer. Both parents grew up like this, as did many of my friends in the village. As was the case in all farming families, we kids worked in the fields during harvest times, especially during the summers to harvest the tulip bulbs; at the time, pre-automation early 1970s, this involved crawling on hands and knees, gathering the bulbs in a wooden box, from 7 a.m. to 6 p.m., six days a week. It was during one of these long days, with only a transistor radio for distraction, that I looked into the distance, past the immense field, saw a highway, and said to myself. "I do not know to where this highway leads. Still, I will be on this road one day to a more adventurous and exciting future". I was 14 or 15 years old, and my mind was made up.

For this plan to work, I needed a way to support myself because I never asked anyone for money. So, at 17, I enrolled in a nursing program at the local Catholic hospital, partially run by nuns. The program involved a 3-month classroom orientation, followed by 3.5 years of full-time, working all shifts and studying 1 week a month. It was common to manage up to 30 patients by myself during a night shift; it was a lot of responsibility requiring organizational skills, quick thinking, and sound judgment. During the 4-year program, I received a modest salary, which was part of my strategy; from the beginning, I had two bank accounts, one checking and one savings, and put half of my salary into my savings account; I never touched the savings, I lived on the other half.

In August 1980, I graduated from the program with a diploma in nursing, some money in the bank, and two nursing school friends who I had convinced to join me in my adventures. We packed our backpacks, got on a train in Hoorn, a small town with a lovely historic train station, waved goodbye to our parents, and were on our way.

Two years earlier, the three of us met two Israeli young men on the train from Paris to Hoorn; we became friends and stayed connected. In 1979, we visited them in Israel, and through them, I met Dov; the visit turned into a summer romance. Because of this, Israel became our destination for the backpacking adventure; we arrived after 4 weeks of train tracking through Europe, going cheap by sleeping in youth hostels, trains, and run-down hotels that went 'by the hour.'

Almost immediately, Dov and I met up again and began dating. At the time, however, I was also dating an Italian guy, and the plan was to go to the Netherlands together over Christmas and get engaged. After all, Dov had only sent me one letter, and we had no contact for almost a year. Well, the plan changed because I made another choice.

I worked in Kibbutz Galil Yam in Herzliya for the first 2 months in Israel. It was great but ultimately not exciting enough, so I made an appointment with the director of nursing at Meir Hospital in Kefar Saba and landed a nursing job for $50 a month, plus housing and food from the hospital kitchen. For the remaining 10 months in Israel, I worked, made friends, went to the beach, and dated Dov . . . it was a wonderful time, and we didn't think, or talk about, anything beyond a week out.

One day Dov shared with me that, even though his friend would not be going to the U.S., he, Dov, was determined to go anyway, and so he would be leaving in the summer to start school in the fall of 1981. Since we hadn't made any promises about any future together, it wasn't my place to do anything other than support him to follow his dreams and begin planning my future. In August 1981, I left Israel, applied for nursing positions in the Netherlands, and accepted one beginning in January 1982. I deliberately delayed the start date because Dov's plans changed somewhat: his father had to undergo open-heart surgery, and he decided to postpone his start date in the U.S. until the spring of 1982. Instead, once his family situation stabilized, he came to visit me for a few months, giving him and my family an opportunity to get acquainted. We traveled some, and Dov played around in real snow for the first time in his life; on December 14, 1981, the day after my 23rd birthday, Dov left for the U.S.

Dov's Intro to the U.S.

Dov

My parents made many friends in the U.S. because my dad was a tour guide working with small groups for extended trips, and through one of them, I landed at George Washington University (GWU) in Washington, D.C.; they invited me to stay with them in their house in the Kalorama district, which was within walking distance of the GWU. Despite all my confidence and bravado about doing this on my own, I was very lonely and had a hard time; being alone in a "strange" country and not mastering the language fluently was hard. So I devised a plan to bring Elma over, something she knew nothing about; remember, no cellphones, no phone calls because of the cost, and only a few letters (we already established that I am a very unreliable letter writer). Every morning I scoured the paper for affordable apartments to rent, circled them, and presented them to my friend in the evening, and he immediately crossed them out. This went on for a few days until one day, I asked him why none of these was a good option. He answered that these were not areas where I could live, and besides, why did I want to leave their basement? I told him about my plan to bring Elma over, he asked for her telephone number, called her right there and then, and told her to come as soon as possible, and to stay with them, because "*Dov was wilting away on the sofa*".

Elma's Intro to the U.S.

Elma

After Dov left on December 14, my parents were relieved, thinking that I had shed my need for adventure, was going to settle down, and possibly marry a nice Dutch Catholic doctor. It was not to be because on December 26, I received a call: black telephone on the wall with a coiled cord, the only phone in the house, and by pure coincidence, I was the only one at home. I picked up the phone, and it was Dov's American friend, with whom he was staying in Washington D.C.: "Are you, Elma? Yes?? . . . So, Dov is here wilting away on the sofa, being all lonely and sad, so I suggest you get on a plane and come here". I was stunned. "Hmmm, OK", I said, and so it went: I announced to my parents that, while they were out visiting family, my plans had changed. I canceled my job, got a visa and a ticket, and, instead of starting my first day on a new job, landed in Washington, D.C., on January 6, 1982. The trip was troubled because of immigration issues, which caused me to stand alone and scared outside at John F. Kennedy Airport at 3:00 a.m., not knowing where to go and what to do, and Dov not knowing where I was and why I didn't arrive in Washington, D.C., as scheduled. Anyway, I found my way to Washington D.C., and from that time, we were together.

January 1982–May 1983

Dov

Life became a little nicer once we were together, but the hard part was yet to come; I needed to register at the university and begin my studies. I must share the story of how this registration went, which is only funny in hindsight.

The process involved walking from desk to desk, set up in a circle in the university gym, meeting with the professors or their deputies, introducing myself, and asking to get registered into their class. Since my bachelor's degree wasn't in computer science, it took some persuasion to be allowed into some of the classes, and since my mastery of English was limited, it took courage. After enrolling in three courses, including the required English 101, I arrived at the last desk, that of the bursar, where I was presented with an invoice for $3,600 dollars. I had read in the catalog that the tuition was $400, so I believed that the total should be $1,200 dollars. I confidently corrected the bursar clerk telling her the 'right' amount,' but after a few back-and-forths, she patiently explained that the tuition listed in the catalog is per credit hour and that each class is three credit hours: $3,600 it was, and we realized that we had enough savings for about a third of a degree. We decided to get started and see what would happen. It never occurred to us to ask our parents, or anyone, for money or loans. We were just going to figure it out along the way. We understood that things were different in the U.S. and that it would take flexibility and resilience to get through it. I began my studies, determined to finish my degree in 18 months somehow.

Elma

Dov began his studies and, with him busy, I needed something to challenge me and a way to make some money. Without a work permit, I was unable to work, and we had no resources for me to study. I did two things: I found work that did not require a permit, like babysitting and working as an in-home aide (making $4.40/hr for 12-hr overnight shifts), and I decided that I had to accomplish "something", so I signed myself up for the State Board of Nursing Licensing Exam in Washington, D.C. To prepare, I went with Dov to the university several mornings a week, and as he went to his classes, I studied the nursing books in the medical library at GWU. I was able to sit for the test only in February of 1983—two 8-hour days of multiple-choice tests—and received the "pass" results in May during the same week that Dov graduated with his MSc in computer science. Our total combined assets were less than $100, but he had his degree, and I had my license to practice nursing.

We had gotten married the year before, on October 16, 1982, with $100 for both wedding rings from a pawn shop, my sister's wedding dress, and a borrowed tie. We served homemade salmon mouse and fruit salad and had the ceremony in front of about 10 people in a friend's house. We were thrifty and cared only about building a future together.

1983–2000

Dov got a job with a small start-up as a developer, and I got my first nursing job at Sibley Hospital in Washington, D.C. We each earned about $35,000/year. We began building the next phase of our life. We planned to eventually settle in either Israel or The Netherlands, but with no resources to our name, any decision about this would have to wait.

The following 10 to 15 years are a blur of mundane but wonderful events: from a rented apartment to a house and then to a bigger house, the arrival of our son, Mark, in 1986 and our daughter, Karyn, in 1988. I continued my education with a bachelor of science in nursing (BSN) and later an master of science in nursing/family nurse practitioner (MSN/FNP). Life was busy and good.

Before Integrated Data Corporation/Dovel

Dov

For most of my professional life, I was a company owner. My first three jobs were as an employee, but I somehow gravitated to start-ups without giving it much thought. Were start-ups in my genes from day one? Could my brain predict the future?

My MS is in computer science with a minor in engineering administration. In May 1983, during the break at my last class, the professor wrote on the board, "We are looking for a software developer". "Hmmm, they're looking for a developer, and I am a developer . . . they have a paying position, and I need an income!" I walked up to the professor and said, "I can do that". He invited me to interview with his two business partners the next day. I impressed them and got my first job at Information Systems Incorporated (ISI).

Information Systems Incorporated

ISI's project was to build a simulation game, called the President Choice, for Apple computers. This game was a SIM City–like game. The player acts as the president of the U.S.: making decisions and gaining or losing popularity to win the midterm and the presidential election. It was a fun project but ahead of its time.

One day the managing partner told me that they needed to reduce my salary because of financial constraints. After talking it over with Elma, I offered to work for free for a few months. They were so impressed that they made me a junior partner. I was so proud, my very first business ownership! Unfortunately, ISI went out of business a few months later due to a lack of funding and being too early in the gaming market. I had gained my first work experience, some income for a while, and the beginnings of a network in the information technology (IT) industry (this comes back later in the book).

Access Engineering Corporation

My next employer was another start-up called Access Engineering Corporation (AEC). The objective of that start-up was to obtain home-meter utility readings over the same phone line used for voice conversations. We wrote software to be placed at the central office of the phone company, separated out the meter reading data, transmitted it to the appropriate utility company (electric/water), and continued the flow of the voice data. We built a working prototype that we deployed, and everything worked. It was very exciting. We could see additional investments in our future; however, it was not to be. At the time, AT&T was a monopoly and ultimately broken up by the courts. Our ability to send both voice and utility data over the same line hinged on this antitrust suit, and couldn't be deployed until the case was completed, which took too long for the company to survive. Another promising start-up became a casualty.

CompuMark U.S.

While at AEC, a dear friend, who was the general manager of an international trademark searching company called CompuMark U.S., called and asked if I knew dBASE III; despite my unfamiliarity with this development language, I said yes with no hesitation, and she asked if I could develop a simple contact management system for CompuMark to manage its customer base. I accepted the assignment. However, since I had a full-time job, I outsourced it to a consultant. I checked in with him on a regular basis and was told that everything was right on track. All seemed well, except . . . it wasn't.

I committed to giving a 5¼-inch disk with the developed work to a CompuMark manager, in time for her to take to her meeting with corporate management at its headquarters in Belgium. On the morning of the day that she was scheduled to fly to Belgium, I arranged to meet the consultant to collect the disk so I could give it to her. I called him to agree on place and time, and he told me that. . . *he had nothing to give me!!* He told me that he had significantly underestimated the scope of the work, thought that he could do it all the night before, and failed. I was stunned. Now what? I couldn't let my friend down, and I had made a promise! I had no choice but to ask Elma to do the one thing she hates most: tell a lie.

Elma called the CompuMark manager and told her that I had been delayed on an out-of-town business trip and couldn't meet her to deliver the disk (remember, this is way before cell phones). Until today I don't know whether she believed it, but I never felt worse. We agreed to postpone the disk delivery by 1 week, but I had to build this system after hours because I still had a day job. For a week, I worked from 9 a.m. to 5 p.m. at AEC and from 5 p.m. to 7 a.m. at home programming in dBase III. Elma was my tester during the day and provided me with a list of issues when I arrived home. It was an efficient process and our first 'business partnership.' I completed and delivered the work as promised and learned a valuable lesson: TRUST BUT VERIFY, which became one of my life principles. Also, I vowed to never again put Elma in a position to be forced to tell a lie.

SCOPE Incorporated

With AEC out of business, I was yet again job seeking. I still did some consulting for CompuMark on the side, but this wasn't enough. I landed at SCOPE Incorporated, whose product was software for an IBM PC board to allow the use of the Defense Data Network (DDN), the predecessor for today's internet; it was exciting work, writing assembly language code for an erasable programmable read-only memory (EPROM) with the objective to ensure efficient code in terms of speed and size; I was good at it and enjoyed it. Until several months later, that division of SCOPE folded, and I was on the street once again. This was the last time I worked for someone else. . . .

Elma

My story during these days isn't nearly as exciting or relevant. In the summer of 1983, we moved out of the friends' basement into a summer house-sitting opportunity. A few months later, we rented a one-bedroom apartment in Falls Church, and in 1985, we bought a house in Reston: a four-bedroom split level on half an acre, for

$108,000! We bought a car, with a friend co-signing the loan; for me, buying a car on credit was unthinkable, but I needed a way to get to my job as a nurse at Sibley Hospital. We paid off the car loan as soon as possible. I worked day and night shifts at Sibley until late 1983 and then transferred to a daytime clinical position at an HMO so I could take classes in the evening. I decided that I would have the same level of education as Dov so that my kids would never think that education was a gender "thing"; this, in addition to university studies being for the elites, had been the culture in which I grew up. In 1985, I started with English 101, and in 1993, I completed my master's degree. I converted to Judaism 3 weeks before Mark was born in March 1986; Karyn was born in September 1988, so I was busy. One day late in 1986, Dov came home from his job at Scope, informed me that his division was folding, and said, "How about we start our own company?"

2

DOVEL IS BORN

How did we get started as entrepreneurs? It wasn't like we were sitting around thinking of a start-up idea, or that this had always been our dream . . . it happened because of the events described earlier, in Chapter 1: circumstances showed us that, if we wanted to "control our destiny" we had to get in the driver's seat. In this chapter, we describe what events led to the "birth" of Dovel and how luck and opportunity met.

DOI: 10.4324/9781003260653-3

Figure 2.1 IDC Logo

Figure 2.2 Dovel Logo

Dov

When I learned that my job at SCOPE was about to end, I was frustrated with the lack of job security in this country (after all, my father worked in the same company his entire adult life) and the fact that I had no control over my destiny. I started talking with a colleague about starting our own company. One day I came home to Elma, who was bathing Mark, and asked her, "What do you think about starting our own company?" and she responded without hesitation, "Sure, that sounds like a good idea". To us, our company meant determining our destiny, so let's go for it!

My colleague and I started Integrated Data Corporation (IDC), a software consulting company. Still, after only a few months, he decided that it wasn't for him and his wife, so he signed over his ownership to me, making me 100% equity holder of IDC! Never mind that IDC had only two employees, no assets, no contracts, and no revenues; we were proud business owners . . . a true immigrant story. We incorporated, opened a bank account, designed a logo and letterhead, and were off and running.

Elma and I are strong supporters of entrepreneurship, but with a word of caution: when you hear entrepreneurs talk about their successful exits, remember that you only see the end product of a long, arduous journey. Building a successful company is a long and complex process, requiring many sacrifices along the way, and should not be underestimated. It can be deceiving to hear stories about a few entrepreneurs meeting in a diner, drawing something on a napkin, and selling the idea for millions of dollars. It happens but. . .

Figure 2.3 Luck

There are two statements we quote in conversations on whether we were just "lucky" much:

You need to open the door to allow luck to enter.
                                                    – David Levy (my father)

Luck is what happens when preparation meets opportunity.
                                        (a sign on a beach café in Tel Aviv)

Yes, of course, luck played a role in our success. However, we still had to make the risky decision to open the door, go through it, and make sure that we were prepared: intellectually, academically, financially, mentally, and much more.

Late 1980s

CompuMark Research Trademark System

One day, our CompuMark friend called me again to ask for my support in the IT department, which wasn't managed well; I agreed to come as a consultant to support their IT department, which led to the development of the CompuMark Research Trademark System. I hired two developers whom I knew from George Washington University, and the three of us completed the project of building a worldwide system. With no internet in the world and only a 300- (and later a 9600-) baud dial-up connection, we designed a sophisticated phonetic algorithm that allowed people to find trademarks based on resemblances.

Electronic Data Gathering and Retrieval System

In January 1989, I received a call from one of the three partners at my first job at ISI. As a true believer in maintaining relationships, I had stayed in touch with him. He had joined BDM (later TRW, and then Northup Grumman [NG]), a prominent government contractor. BDM had won a contract to build a mission-critical system for the Securities and Exchange Commission, called the Electronic Data Gathering Analysis and Retrieval (EDGAR) system, and it was looking for high-tech people. The program manager asked him for "the best programmer you know", and he called me. I managed a group of developers for this project, and we built the EDGAR system. This was the beginning of a long relationship between IDC/Dovel and BDM/TRW/NG and between the PM and Dov and Elma.

A Door Opens. . .

The EDGAR project was staffed with many subcontractors, an administrative burden to the BDM accounting team. The PM was lamenting this to me one day, and I recognized an opportunity: IDC could consolidate all these entities on one contract and send BDM one invoice. Wow! With one stroke, IDC's contract grew from one subcontractor to 20! We added a 5% handling fee, which became the starting capital and cash flow for the future company.

After EDGAR came a program with BDM involving building the blood system for the American Red Cross, and in the late 1990s, IDC got involved with the Defense Travel System (DTS): that's when the significant changes happened!

DTS

I was having a grand time sprinkling wisdom as the chief technology officer of the American Red Cross when I received a call from

BDM/TRW asking me to come and talk to them about the DTS program. It was soon clear to me that this was a troubled program and that the wisest thing for me to do was find the nearest exit. I did not.

At its request, I gathered a team and assessed the program, which validated my earlier impression. I delivered an excellent scathing report, including some recommendations, and wished them luck.

This program was very costly to BDM, and it needed help. Still, I knew how hard it would be to turn this disaster around (even the program logo – a picture of a train, plane, and automobile – was pointing backward). I didn't have the mental energy for another large system development program. I declined their initial offer, but everyone has their price, and they came with an offer I couldn't refuse.

Turning this program around was even more challenging than I had anticipated, but it provided us with an opportunity to take IDC to the next level. As a DoD program, clearances were required, and for people to be cleared, they had to be employed by a company with a facility clearance . . . and that, as our friend the PM would say, is when IDC became a "real company"!

Elma

January 2000

Timing and opportunity met at the beginning of the new century; not only was there a need for change at IDC/Dovel, but the possibility also presented itself at the perfect time for me.

Dov was well aware of my hesitation about going into business together, so he approached me from a direction he knew would be effective: he told me about the opportunity for IDC and that, if we were going to take this on, someone needed to "build and own" the corporate infrastructure – if not me, then someone else. He knew that this would work because I am fiercely independent and would not want an outsider managing our family business, including our income distributions and taxes.

It was perfect timing, because at the time, we had bought a very old house that required extensive renovation, had sold our house before we were able to move into the house under renovation, and had to live in an apartment for about 8 months, which required significant coordination. In addition, I was between jobs, looking for a change in my health care career. One day I told Dov about a teaching position for which I was considered when we realized that this was all going to be way too much: renovating, selling a house, moving, new job, Dov working 16 hours days, managing a changing IDC, and keeping the family sane and together. Time to reshuffle priorities. I reluctantly agreed to postpone my career for 4 to 6 months to focus on all the other demands.

Part II

LESSONS LEARNED

3

BUILDING THE CORPORATE INFRASTRUCTURE

As Dovel's CEO, Elma implemented a plan for scaling the corporate infrastructure. Later, as a leadership coach and business mentor, Elma works with entrepreneurs and shares her 'lessons learned'. In this chapter she describes how business decisions around investing in organizational resources, such as leases, systems, and staff, are complex decisions. Overinvesting can result in liabilities that burden the company, while underinvesting may leave the organization unable to support operations as rapid growth happens.

Whether a current increase in work means a sustained upward growth curve or a temporary surge, determines what you do next concerning investing and hiring.

As you scale, there are many variables to consider:

- How to estimate what systems you need
- How to build in checks and balances as the teams grow
- How to determine if an investment is worthwhile making
- How to price your services (or products) so that sales cover direct cost, indirect cost, and profit

As we built Dovel and positioned it for growth, we learned the necessity of building an organizational infrastructure that was stable enough to provide structure, flexible enough to allow for growth, and resilient enough to withstand challenges and the test of time.

DOI: 10.4324/9781003260653-5

Elma

Let me start by describing a business concept that I wish I had known during the growing and scaling phases of Dovel: The Phases of The Organizational Life Cycle. This is not something invented by me, I wish! Instead, it is widely described and discussed in the business literature. My advice, "read up on it"; it will give you a framework for understanding where you and your organization are, what to accept as usual 'behavior,' and what to anticipate. Like a parenting guide, not everything described in the concept fits you and your situation, but you will recognize the similarities in big lines.

I use this framework to discuss the scaling of Dovel and use our personal experiences as an illustration.

There are multiple versions of this in the literature; the one that most resonates with me is the following:

- Start-up
- Growth: early growth to rapid growth
- Maturity: the slowdown of growth or no growth
- Renewal or Death

2000–2005: THE START-UP PHASE

Mission Statement

A start-up company is not the baby version of a large, fully matured company despite the common perception. Instead, it is an "organization" (sometimes consisting of no more than two people) in search of a working business model; the founder(s) have ambition, a rough idea of a mission, and somewhat of a plan on how to achieve that mission. Without those three elements, it will be challenging to achieve anything. I used to "pooh-pooh" the whole concept of "mission" and considered it just talk without adding any value to what we were trying to do. But when we developed a basic website, it needed content, including a description of "what we are about", so one rainy Sunday afternoon, I sat down and wrote *The Mission Statement*. That's when I recognized the importance of articulating and socializing the company's mission. Once you get the mission statement down, it becomes the guiding light for corporate decision-making: every investment and effort is measured by if and how it supports the company's mission. Writing the company's mission statement in concise language is not simple; it requires one to think about what you, the founder(s), believe is the company's purpose and mission. Once you get it right, it needs to be socialized with the team to help everyone stay focused. If your mission statement is short and straightforward, it should be a byline on the corporate letterhead and in every team member's email signature.

- Your mission statement should answer the question, What does XYZ do?
  - Answer: the mission of XYZ is "to develop', 'to facilitate', 'to create', and so on.

Two examples illustrate the importance of socializing your company's mission.

At some point during the very early phase of Dovel, when I was still working alone, with Maggy, my golden retriever, in the attic of our home, we hired someone who had been an executive at a venture-backed start-up to develop a business teaming opportunity. He was used to a nice office, a secretary, a suite at the local stadium, and so on, you get the idea, and he didn't like our corporate "setup" in the attic. Rather than focusing on the opportunity we hired him for, he connected with corporate real estate agents to get "real office space", began complaining about having to do administrative tasks himself, and wanted a secretary. We understood where he was coming from; we knew that his previous employer was a start-up that blew through several millions of venture capital funding without ever actually achieving anything before it went bankrupt. In our case, however, we did not have any outside funding because all the investments came from Dov and Elma, and we were careful with our spending. I asked him, "How does an office/secretary/box suite support our mission and bring revenues?" And, of course, he had no answer to this. This is not to say that these investments are never needed, but it depends on your company, what you sell and to whom, and what phase you are in the organizational life cycle. At a much later stage of maturity, it might be essential to make these investments; I describe this later in this chapter, but be sure that you can justify your spending by answering the question, "Does this support our mission?"

Later, Dovel had a business development (BD) team tasked with bringing in and developing opportunities for new business. As almost all founders know (or will learn), during the start-up/rapid growth phase, nearly all new business comes from the founder/entrepreneur(s) through relationships; however, this is not scalable, and at some point, this responsibility needs to go to a BD team. Inevitably, to be successful in bringing in new business, the BD team will veer off course and present opportunities that are not related to the core expertise of the company or its mission. And so it happened that we, as management, were given, and ultimately made the mistake of competing for, an opportunity that was solely in the wheelhouse of the VP of BD: a contract to develop a continuity of operations plan. We won the competitive RFP (request for proposal) process, which was significant; however, other than the vice president (VP) of BD, there were no resources with the skill sets for this work. This caused problems across all departments. We needed to hire help with skills sets that would not be billable full-time (FT), nor was this an opportunity to expand our presence in this agency as this was not a program in which we could show our core competencies. Minor problems became big problems, and ultimately, the VP of BD walked away with the customer connection, which we allowed to happen because we recognized that we should never have been there to begin with. Overall, it caused significant turmoil, as is always the case in a small organization, and in looking back, we knew that this could have been avoided if we had asked the right question: Is this work aligned with our mission?

You will read more about this, and about the challenges that come with this in Chapter 8 by Dov: "Chasing Rabbits".

The Start-Up Phase: Scaling

Now that we have the mission statement, let's talk about the start-up "organization". There are several characteristics that define the start-up phase: controlled chaos, an undefined business model, undefined roles and responsibilities, few processes, and a culture of camaraderie and "we're in this together". It's fun, it's exhausting, and it's ultimately also not sustainable. Suppose you are the sole person responsible for the corporate infrastructure. In that case, as I was, you will quickly find yourself on a speeding treadmill, unable to keep up yet unable to slow down and hire the support you know you need. Even if you do, you don't take (or have) the time to carefully vet the support, nor do you have the funds to bring in an overhead person. Finally, it's hard to give the responsibility of many tasks to someone else, someone you do not yet know or trust.

There isn't enough space in this chapter to write a complete textbook with advice on what to do and what not to do, so, after carefully thinking about how to write this chapter, I decided to describe a few lessons learned, illustrated with some examples of what went well, what I could have done better and what I now, in hindsight, would not recommend. I must admit that it's uncomfortable to expose "how the sausage was made" during the early phases of Dovel, but then again, *all's well that ends well*, right?

I took on organizing the corporate infrastructure, thinking that this would take 4 to 6 months, after which I fully intended to pick up my health care career again. So, without thinking and planning too much, I dove in headfirst. Perhaps this was for the best because overthinking it at the time would likely have resulted in fear and inaction; after all, I had no idea what I was doing. I had to learn Excel and MS Word and didn't know anything about government contracting, accounting, finance, overhead (OH)/general and administrative (G&A), and more.

This is where the immigrant spirit of *"can do"* was helpful; whether backpacking through Europe, working in Israel, moving to the U.S., getting licensed, obtaining a BSN/MSN, becoming a nurse practitioner, or agreeing to partner with my husband to build a business, I never spend too much time and energy overthinking it. Instead, my philosophy was (and still is)

1. I think to myself: what is the worst that can happen.
2. I visualize the worst outcome and what I can do to address/solve it.
3. I no longer worry because I now have a plan on what to do in the worst-case scenario (which, by the way, usually does not materialize).

It seems simplistic, but it worked for me throughout my Dovel years. . . .

Anyway, here are some lessons learned from the start-up phase.

There were two corporate areas where I knew I needed to put my focus first:

*   Finance and accounting
*   Strategic corporate relationships (banking, accounting, legal)

Not that everything else wasn't necessary, but if I didn't have "a handle" on the numbers, nothing else would matter. If I didn't have relationships with a team of experts who would have my back in a time of need, I would find myself at a loss when I needed the most support. So, here's a short description:

Finance and Accounting

a. **Create a simple budget!**
    I cannot emphasize this enough! I took a one-day workshop to learn government contracting accounting and developed a simple budget; I used that as a baseline to monitor our

revenues' growth and profit. It is straightforward to think that you are too small to have a budget, or you have to have a perfect budget designed by an accountant (and that's expensive). Still, my advice is that you just get started with a very simple ledger that lists revenues, direct expenses, such as cost of goods sold, and indirect expenses, such as OH and G&A; it doesn't have to be perfect, but it's important not to overthink it and to get started with something simple and improve it over time. You will use this budget as a guide for the following year's budget and get better at it every time. We reviewed the financials monthly, analyzed the variances, and, if needed, adjusted. The earlier you get into doing this, the more comfortable you will be with your financials. Even though I started out knowing absolutely nothing about financials, and I didn't know how to use Excel, I quickly learned how and what to do and that I liked "this stuff".

b. **Develop your pricing**

You will need the budget to develop your "rates" if you sell services or "product price" for products. There is enough information in the business literature about pricing formulas and rate buildups, and there isn't enough room in this chapter to write up a complete course on this, but here are a few essential points:

Failure to use a pricing methodology, including anticipating indirect costs, can cause you to lose money. It may appear that you are doing well; after all, revenues and sales are up, so what's the problem? The problem is that if you haven't developed your "rates" based on a reasonable budget, you may be losing money with every sale.

I retained the services of a wonderful retired Defense Department Audit Agency (DCAA) consultant, who came twice a year to work with me on developing the buildup (aka the rates or the load). In addition to pricing, I used these rates as a measure to track our expenses.

Develop your pricing for "the company you plan to be" 1 to 2 years out; you may have an escalation rate in your contract, but it may not be enough to cover your indirect costs as you scale your organization or as your direct cost escalates. Your final cost per item (product or billable hour) will consist of the direct cost, fringe/OH/G&A, and fee (which is your profit). Pricing is tricky because you will not be competitive if you price too high, and too low will result in losing money.

Watch your expenses!!

As the owners of a start-up with no third-party funding, it was essential for us to be prudent about how we spent our money. We decided that we did not want any additional equity stakeholders, as we preferred to remain independent without considering other decision-makers. Aside from a reasonable salary, all net income was reinvested in the company. This is where my cultural background of frugality, and a conservative approach to spending, came into play; in hindsight, my penny-pinching may have held us back somewhat from faster growth and development. Because of my Dutch upbringing, I refused to carry debt or have unnecessary loans. (The Dutch word for *debt* is *guilt*, so it's culturally ingrained in me). I diligently asked myself: Does this support the mission for all business expenses? Is this needed for growth and development?

c. **Get a Line of Credit**

Despite my dislike of loans and liabilities, I recognized that there would be times when cash flow is challenged, that is, when invoices are paid late, when there are unexpected expenses, or when there is a sudden surge in team hires to staff a project (you will need to pay them before you get paid), so we established a line of credit (LOC) with a bank. Because we were the sole owners of Dovel, and the company did not have sufficient collateral assets, we were forced to sign a personal liability clause. Even though we had significant risk tolerance, we didn't like it because if things took a turn, we could lose everything we had built over the years, and we still had kids to put through college. When people see us now, after we have enjoyed a successful exit, they do not see the risks we had to take. Still, we did what we had to do and continued to be careful with our money. The LOC, or loan, is something you want to establish when your financials look strong because when you need it, your company's situation may look different, and you may have difficulty getting a bank to work with you.

Strategic Corporate Relationships

You need to invest time and money in resources early on because not doing so can be very costly and painful when things go sideways (and they will at some point or another). For me, those resources were *banking*, *accounting*, and *legal support*. I knew that should I need either of those at the spur of the moment, it would be essential to have existing relationships that enabled me to call them with "an ask", and they would know our company and me.

Banking

I do not recall how I met my contact at Bank of America, but he became my trusted banking advisor. Since we were cautious with our money, we didn't need much in terms of loans, other than our LOC, but he would check in from time to time; when, much later, we had our first acquisition, he was there . . . he knew us, and it was an easy conversation.

Accounting

We started with our accountant, whom I liked very much; however, we quickly outgrew her. Again, we moved to a slightly larger firm, very personable, and we developed genuine relationships. It was valuable to call or email my accountant with a quick question because she knew the company and me well. After a few years, we realized that we had to move to an accounting firm with Government Contracting expertise. We ultimately moved to Argy, Wiltse (later BDO); the BDO team became my support and continues to be until today. Everyone in the office knew that Elma would not make accounting 'moves' without checking with "her BDO Team" first!

Legal

For legal as well, we started with our attorney but quickly moved to a firm experienced in government contracting. We asked around and were advised to contact Andy Lustig at Cooley. Andy and, later, Aaron Binstock are our corporate legal counsel until this day. Last year, at lunch, to celebrate the sale of our company, Andy and Aaron suggested that we write this book, and they made the introduction to a literary agent, so if you read this, you have them to thank for it.

What these resources have in common is that we developed long-term, invaluable relationships with each of them; until today, this is the team I can call on for advice, support, and help. They know me, they know Dov, and they know Dovel. It is vital that you feel comfortable with and trust your strategic resources team. Before Argy/BDO, we retained another accounting firm, and I quickly realized it was no trusting relationship, so I changed within a year and found what I was looking for. My advice: don't settle until you see "your team", and once you do, make sure you develop *and maintain* relationships!

OK, these are the essential nuggets to think of during the start-up phase. So what did Dovel look like during this time, which was somewhere between 1 and 5 years? Many mistakes, trials and errors, and worries but also excitement and pride.

During the Start-Up Phase

Dovel was called IDC (Integrated Data Corporation), and it was very much a lifestyle company. We did not have investors because we wanted to retain independence. IDC/Dovel was a woman-owned small business (WOSB) with a 49%/51% ownership structure. We never took competitive advantage of the WOSB status. Still, it was helpful as it allows large primes (the company that holds the contract with the government) to use that set-aside status to fulfill their requirement to provide some percentage of the work to a company with a WSOB status. Set-aside status means that a contract can be awarded without competition.

Corporate HQ was initially in the attic of our home in Bethesda, where I spend my time, initially with our golden retriever, Maggy, and later with additional office support. Then, as we added office staff, we moved to a "shared corporate office space" and, in 2005, when we outgrew that arrangement, we signed our first lease, a 5-year considerable commitment in Tysons Corner.

After the first 12 months of managing an increasingly unmanageable workload, I hired a part-time office assistant, which soon became a full-time position and a recruiter. I was human resources (HR), contracting, accounting, and everything else; I remember being perpetually exhausted, trying to be the perfect everything to everybody. Although Dov and I had made clear agreements about our "swim lanes", there were unavoidable conflicts, especially when someone on "my team" wasn't sufficiently supportive of someone on "his team". We worked it out, however, and usually avoided work conversations during family time.

Business Processes

Once more than one person is involved in the business's corporate governance, there is a need to develop Business Processes to ensure efficiency, avoid gaps and overlaps, secure oversight, and begin building a flexible yet strong foundation for continued scaling. The objective is to find the balance between delegating and micromanaging; unlike its common perception, delegation is not "telling someone what to do"; instead, it is to give someone the responsibility, the *ownership*, of a certain outcome; the way this is done is not the most important since there are many ways to get to a desirable outcome. My rule was to do it "my way or better" . . . if you don't have a better way, you might as well do it my way, but at the end of the day, it's about the outcome. I do have to admit, though, that this was not easy because it requires "letting go" (see also the chapter on letting go). It must not have been easy to work for me because, mainly due to fatigue and feeling overwhelmed, I was often impatient. I know that I could have done a better job mentoring and guiding. I am writing this with the benefit of hindsight and increased maturity.

Over time, I was able to hand over much of the administrative work to an F/T assistant, who served as office manager and managed accounts receivable (AR)/accounts payable (AP) and most of the HR generalist functions. We managed all financials on Quick-Books (QB), a system I was comfortable and familiar with.

Sometime during the second year, we progressed from paper/faxed timesheets to Replicon's Canadian timesheet system. After dealing with the inconsistency and inefficiency of paper, this was an enormous improvement since it provided audit trails and history. We were able to do away with the paper timesheets. Invoices were manually prepared in Excel and submitted in pdf format; payments were received as checks via the regular "snail mail" and deposited in the bank.

Initially, all staff worked on a 1099/contracting basis, so there was no need for payroll or fringe benefits; they would submit an invoice for hours worked, and we paid the invoice net 30 days; I was very precise with paying on time, as I understood that they, too, had bills to pay. I remember very clearly when a considerable payment from our client got lost in the mail for several weeks. This significantly impacted our cash flow, but, at the time, we did not have an LOC in place yet. We temporarily had to float our funds so that everyone could get paid. This minor incident taught me that we needed an LOC fast.

Facility Clearance

During that same year, we were asked to obtain "facility clearance" status to place "cleared" employees on the contract. Although it was an opportunity for us, it meant that we both had to give up our citizenship because the founders, as the "roots" of the facility clearance, could only be American citizens.

Dov had dual American/Israeli citizenship and gave up his Israeli citizenship. I had European (Dutch) citizenship and an American "Green Card"; Dutch rules did not permit dual citizenship, and I never wanted to give it up, so, for almost 20 years, "Green Card" status was fine with me. However, I gave up my Dutch citizenship, which was very hard for me, and became an American citizen. I had to pass a few tests before I was approved for citizenship. On the day of "Naturalization", the whole family (we kept the kids home from school for this unusual experience) went to Baltimore for the "Oath Taking Ceremony". It was bittersweet, but we were sure that it was temporary; however, I only have American citizenship to today.

Facility clearance status meant that we could submit staff for security clearances if they were employees of IDC/Dovel. I needed to make some changes: I signed up with Paychex for payroll and worked with a broker to put together a fringe benefit package. I wanted to make sure that our employees knew that we cared about their well-being, so I put together a generous package that included health, short-term/long-term disability, and life insurance, paid for by the company. We offered a simple IRA plan that I managed myself, but we later changed this to a 401K. We had to have at least three employees sign up for these fringe benefits, and we were two. Contractors were not eager to join such a small team without knowing what the benefits would look like, so it became a catch-22 situation . . . until Elliot joined us: he was our first employee other than the two of us, and it was exciting. Elliot worked for IDC/Dovel for a few years, left for another opportunity, and returned later. Now, 20 years later, he is still an employee of Dovel. Around that time, Greg also joined us, and he and Elliot were the

VPs of the Dovel. Dov and I appreciated their confidence in us because the company was very small, with one contract, and we were still working to figure it all out.

In addition to payroll and fringe benefits, we needed to have policies and procedures, so I set out to write those myself. I started with the most basic—"intentional misrepresentation on timesheets is cause for immediate dismissal"—and went from there to policies about showing up at work intoxicated, against harassment, and guidance on paid time off. Regarding the policy on showing up drunk, I honestly thought it ridiculous even to have to write a policy on this, until someone showed up after lunch at the customer site, intoxicated; because we had a written policy, we were able to dismiss him; after all, he acted "against policy". (Ridiculous, right? I know.)

Culture

Parties

In Chapter 4, "Bagels of Friday", I describe how relationships played a significant role at all stages during IDC/Dovel's life cycle; developing and maintaining relationships is something that comes naturally to both of us. During the start-up phase, we needed to know everyone on the team and know their spouses and kids. We had picnics and pool parties at our home during those first few years and holiday parties in the Morrison House in Alexandria, Virginia. We made it a point to greet everyone as they came, and I memorized the names of the spouses. A few people joined our team during these early years and are still with us; we know their spouses and hear about the kids growing up and going off to college. These close relationships also meant that people felt comfortable coming to us asking for help; we gave loans so people could keep their kids in a special school, put a down payment on a home they wanted, or get the cosmetic dentistry treatment they needed but couldn't afford. We kept these incidences very confidential, but it was a wonderful feeling that they felt comfortable asking us and that we could support them. It became harder to stay connected with everyone as we grew, something we regretted.

iPads

The first iPads came out much later, and we wanted to do something special for the team; by that time, our team size was about 60 to 70 strong. So, we ordered 70 iPads and engraved them with the Dovel logo. One day we ordered pizza and asked everyone to come to the meeting/breakfast/lunchroom. When everyone was seated and had their slice, we rolled in a cart with 70 brown cardboard boxes, each labeled with a name, and we began handing out the boxes. Initially, nobody knew what to do, so we urged them to open the boxes . . . we will never forget the faces once they realized that these were actual iPads! It was such a wonderful vibe of excitement, and it made us so happy.

Washington Capitals (CAPS)

Dov and I were season ticket holders of the Washington Capitals, the CAPS; it was a lot of fun to go to the games, even though they never really made it to the Stanley Cup until 17 years into our CAPS tenure. We wanted to share this excitement with the team, so at the beginning of each hockey season, Dov created an Excel spreadsheet and allowed everyone to get four tickets to a game; these were excellent club seats, and people loved it. I remember one time fondly when an employee went to a game with his family, his wife, and two young sons. The next day, the boys drew a picture of their experience, and the employee sent it to us. I was so moved. This was priceless. Now, at least 15 years later, I still remember how wonderful it felt to provide these experiences.

Figure 3.1 The CAPS were an integral part of Dovel

Community Involvement

Over the years, the Dovel team did its part in giving back to the community through various involvements, such as collections of money, toys, and goods, as well as mentoring of residents, for HomeStretch, a local community organization with programs that lead homeless families to empowerment and independent living, as well as the annual walk for the Susan Komen Foundation. At the yearly 5K walk/run for the Prevent Cancer Foundation, Dovel often was recognized for having the largest participation!

DCAA

In the beginning, our only contract was DTS (Defense Travel System), a large subcontract to Northrup Grumman (NG). Sometime during that first year, while we were still in the attic, NG requested that the DCAA, the auditing agency for this contract, conduct an audit on our records. "Okidoki . . . what on earth is this?" On the day the auditor came over, we stationed her at the dining room

Figure 3.2 Dovel at the Prevent Cancer Event

table while Maggy was banned to the backyard because the auditor was afraid of dogs. We waited for her requests, mainly timesheets, to back up the invoices and contractual validation of the bill rates. I can't say that this first DCAA audit went off without a wrinkle . . . in fact, she gave us a list of items to correct, and she'd be back in 3 months. This turned out the best learning experience for me; I learned exactly what DCAA would be looking for in terms of records, so I organized, filed, and archived accordingly. From that experience on, all subsequent audits have been spotless, and we received compliments on our record keeping. What I learned from this is (a) auditors are not out to get you; in fact, my DCAA consultant later told me that the auditors look for deliberate misrepresentation or gross mismanagement, but if they see that you're making a genuine attempt to do the right thing, they will help you. (b) An audit should be considered a learning experience, so keep an open mind and look forward to audits.

Business development (BD)

Our corporate structure was sound enough to absorb growth towards the end of the start-up phase, but we still had only one (sub) contract. We realized that we needed to add contracts to dilute the risk and provide our team with career opportunities. Dov was busy on the contract, I was busy doing everything corporate, and we didn't have the time to focus on BD. We were very fortunate to have a close friendship and business relationship with a real giant in the government contracting world: Bill McQuiggan. Bill was my business mentor from the beginning and provided me with practical matters, as well as a listening ear when I needed one. We convinced Bill to become our CEO for 1 year, during which the focus was to add one or more prime contracts. He was retired and an avid fisherman, so it took some convincing. Not only did we gain immediate credibility with Bill as our CEO during that year, but we also gained two contracts at the Food and Drug Administration (FDA): our first prime contract, Recall Enterprise System (RES), and the Emergency Operations Network Incident Management System (EON IMS). We still fondly remember these days, when Dov and I, together with other team members, worked all night to meet the proposal deadline, created the three-ring binders, boxed them, taped them up, and hand-delivered them to the contracting officer at the FDA in Rockville. We were so very proud!!

How We Got Our First Prime Contract

Dov

Even though we held only one subcontract, DTS, with one customer, NG, we continued growing and did well financially in the early beginnings. But then we began thinking ahead and realized that we needed a strategy on "how this story ends". The subcontract was for 5 years, and one option was to run it out and call it a day; however, we realized that our team would recognize the lack of career future and, rightfully so, look for opportunities elsewhere; the key people would be the first to go, and without them, the company could not fulfill its obligation. So that strategy wasn't going to work. The only other path was to grow and add contracts outside NG, specifically, prime contracts.

As you can see from the following story, winning a prime contract took luck, preparation, and significant hard work.

IDC had a small subcontract to the FDA, with one person on the contract. Elma describes how this contract came about in her chapter on Relationships. One day this team member told me about the challenges his FDA program manager (PM) had with how a large contractor was implementing Capability Maturity Model Integration (CMMI). As the technical director for DTS, I had credibility because I was very familiar with CMMI and knew how to deliver practical, mission-critical systems. So I asked for an introduction.

During the first meeting with the PM, as he shared his frustrations, I came prepared and talked to him about "compassionate CMMI": using CMMI to improve delivery rather than a way to delay delivery. Two more meetings followed in which he showed me what he had: "binders with artifacts but no system", he kept saying. A few weeks later, an RFP came out; I knew this was our opportunity. We expected competition from larger, more established contractors, and the only way to beat the competition was on price. As a small start-up company, competitive pricing was our advantage, and we were going to use that to win. Our proposal made it through the first review, after which there was an oral presentation. We hired a coach and rehearsed until everything was polished; we won our first prime contract at the FDA!!

The start-up phase is exhausting; it's organized chaos and exhilarating all simultaneously. The camaraderie, team spirit, and "we're all in this together" atmosphere are priceless but ultimately not sustainable.

Sometime in the fourth year, after we gained the two prime contracts, and Bill was our CEO, we recognized that we were needed to make changes to allow for and absorb growth. With the benefit of hindsight, we recognize that we entered to next phase.

2005–2010: THE GROWTH PHASE
Office Space
Elma

The growth phase is a period of constant adjustment to expansion as contracts are added, revenues, and expenses, grow, and the team size increases. One of the most complex decisions to make is about office space: how much space, duration of the lease, location. . . ? A wrong decision has consequences. When we recognized that the shared office space arrangement no longer served us, both financially and organizationally, we looked around for new space. This was completely new territory for us, and we had to learn about lease terms, tenant improvements (TIs), and more. What I learned quickly is to pay attention to details, for example:

- Six months' "free rent" does not mean "six months' free rent"; the rent that's abated is usually added to the end of the lease, at the escalated rate! That's not to say that the cash-flow benefit isn't worth it, but it's essential to know that the total rent will need to be paid. The term *free rent* was banned from the conversations once I learned this little detail.
- For accounting: in the event of "free rent": even though no cash may be paid, the total value of the entire lease is spread over the whole lease period, so the monthly expense is recognized on the books, whether the cash goes out or not.
- Negotiating TIs: how much TI per square foot, what is included (like IT hardware, wiring, etc.).
- The start date of the lease: make sure you understand when the lease begins and ends, as it isn't pleasant to carry double-lease expenses.

So we signed a 5-year lease and moved to Tysons Corner, on Jones Branch Drive, where we leased half of the bottom-lobby level; we acquired the furniture from the previous tenant and made minimal changes. This was our first real space, and we didn't see

Figure 3.3 2005: The first Dovel signage on our first-floor office in
Tysons Corner

the need to renovate or purchase fancy furniture. Over the weekend, Dov and I went with a step ladder, a hammer, and nails to
hang some artwork and whiteboards; we were so proud of this
next step. Soon we put our name on the building . . . wow! We
stood there and watched it coming up. Within a year, we outgrew
the space, and we renegotiated the lease and added the other side
of the lobby. Two years later, we added space on the second floor.

This is an excellent place to recognize and thank Liat Nave,
Dov's sister and a professional graphic designer, for creating the
Dovel logo. We all felt unspeakable pride, seeing the logo on the
buildings and knowing that she was the creative mind behind it.

From QB to MS Navision

To continue preparing for growth, business processes had to scale
as well. Even though I was very comfortable with the QB software,
looking ahead, it was clear to me that this system was not sufficient
for *the company we planned to be a year later*. It wasn't robust,

and more importantly, it wasn't DCAA-compliant (at the time). I asked around, did my homework, and settled on a Microsoft system called Microsoft Navision. This was a significant step: first, it was a significant financial investment. Second, I had to leave my QB comfort zone, but we were now able to bid on RFPs with a DCAA-compliant accounting system requirement. I recovered from the angst of the large spending and realized that this was a critical investment, hired a fantastic young accounting major right out of school, and sent her to training on the system, and, once the system was up and running, we submitted a significant proposal to the FDA, with us as the prime and a team of 10 subs, and we won!! The investment was worthwhile.

I went to MS Navision training, but I didn't have time for the learning curve, and I had complete confidence in our accounting staff. This meant that I had to develop a method for oversight; no longer could I review every detail because I just didn't have the time for it, so I reviewed the financials monthly, and once or twice a month, I would select a random area and go deep into the detail.

JIRA Software

Soon the corporate team consisted of an office manager, an HR director, accounting staff, and a recruiter. For this team to work together seamlessly, especially when it came to recruiting and hiring, involved many yellow 'stickies' on desktop monitors. As a person obsessed with efficiency and organization, this bothered me, but I didn't know how to tackle it. At one time, I developed a RACI chart (a tool that defines who is Responsible, Accountable, Consulted, or Informed for a task or area of work). Still, although it helped bring some organization, the "stickies" remained.

In management meetings, I usually did not pay much attention when the conversations were about software systems as I didn't think it pertained to "my domain"; however, one day, in a senior management meeting, someone talked about the JIRA system, and something about this piqued my interest. JIRA is a software solution used for issue tracking and project management. I thought that it could be a solution for business process management, so I worked with one of the technical managers and put it to work. It wasn't easy to change old habits: I had to mention multiple times that I did not want to see any more yellow stickies, but ultimately, the system solved a business problem and resulted in efficiency, streamlining, and auditable record trails.

BD During the Growth Phase

With the corporate infrastructure solid and resilient enough to absorb growth, the main task during this organizational life cycle is to create growth. This is easier said than done. Initially, during what is considered the "rapid growth phase", most, if not all, new work comes from relationships with existing customers. Most relationships involve the founder. In our case, Dov was well known and recognized for his technical expertise and deep understanding of large, mission-critical systems. The problem with this approach is (a) it's not scalable and (b) the customer wants Dov to be managing the project FT. Dov cannot be everywhere FT, although we joked about cloning him, so we had to hire unknown leadership for "new" work. Sometimes this worked out well, and a team was very successful in making the customer happy, which then gave us a good chance for follow-on work; other times, it didn't work out so well, and not only was the program not successful, but we also didn't establish the kind of reputation and relationships that supported additional growth with that customer.

During the 5-year growth phase, multiple BD directors came and went, none of them successfully created growth, which was very frustrating, disrupting, and expensive. Dovel did expand to multiple agencies, as expansion happened through existing customer relationships and competitive efforts: submitting proposals in response to RFPs. Dovel was a "small business", and much of the work was "small business set-aside", other work was a sub to primes, and some was F&O (full and open), with the latter being the most important, valuable and desirable.

Project Management Reviews

A significant component of maturing and scaling is creating oversight without micromanaging. We established a pattern of monthly project management reviews (PMRs), at which management presented their project status to senior management. The PMRs were very organized and included reviews of financials (funding, profit, growth), quality, customer relations, and more. We paid lots of attention to red flags and created action items. It was an excellent method to oversee without micromanaging and hold project managers accountable for the outcome. I made a Measurement & Analysis manual with key performance metrics, which we used for the PMRs; this manual received a special commendation at the 3-year CMMI L3 assessments.

CMMI

CMMI is a process model that defines what an organization should do to promote behaviors that lead to improved performance.

We recognized that, increasingly, an RFP would ask for a company to have CMMI Level 3 (L3; there are five levels), and lacking this qualification meant an inability to participate, so we decided that Dovel should obtain the CMMI L3 qualification. This was a significant undertaking, which was entirely on the project level and, therefore, in my mind, not something I needed to worry about. Dov and another senior manager at Dovel were familiar with CMMI through their involvement at the DTS program, but they were both FT busy on the contract, so a consultant was hired. This consultant wandered the hallways for a few weeks, with nobody knowing what exactly he was doing; he had everyone sit through an hour of training, and I don't think anyone understood what he was talking about, but the problem was, nobody "owned" this effort. We were all too busy to pay attention. Inevitably, this imploded: we hired a company to do a "dry run" assessment, and we came out of this draft assessment with mud on our faces.

We regrouped and prepared differently by putting in our hard work of documenting processes, creating artifacts, educating our team, and socializing the concept of CMMI. One of the difficulties was that the team had a hard time accepting CMMI as an organized way to do their work; instead, the common complaint was "you want us to do all the project work, and then after that, you want us to do CMMI"; it required a lot of educating and socializing.

Anyway, we asked the same company to come and do another draft assessment, and we were approved for the accurate assessment. When we learned that we were successfully assessed at CMMI L3, we all gathered in the conference room, and we brought in a big cake that said *CMMI!*

Lesson Learned: preparing for a CMMI assessment cannot be done "on the side" by a consultant who is not familiar with the company's processes, and it cannot be done in a hurry overnight. Lesson 2: change is hard!

Personal Challenges

The CMMI L3 helped us somewhat to be able to submit proposals in response to RFPs, but it was frustrating and very much "two steps forward and one back". During this time, we hired a senior VP who interviewed well but, soon after his hire, turned out to be a bad fit. He created tension and an "us-against-them culture" within the team. I did not know how to handle this and tried my usual moderating, accommodating, and reasoning approach, but all this just made things worse. During this time, my father was terminally ill with lung cancer, and I had to be in The Netherlands as much as I could. After he passed away, I went through a challenging period during which I mourned the loss of my father, the climate in the office was toxic, growth was challenging, and Dov and I were not on the same page because he did not see what was happening in the office, nor did he believe me when I told him. I still have a visceral reaction when I think of these 14 months. We almost lost the company as well as each other. This episode is described again in Chapter 5, "Marriage and Business Partnerships".

This very painful period turned out to be a blessing in disguise: because the atmosphere in the office was hard to take, I started to go out of the office to networking events, representing Dovel, becoming "the face of Dovel". I thank our then HR director for this; he came to me one morning and said, "Elma, you need to go out of the office and network"; this was very hard for me because I had been in the office for several years, with Dov doing the "customer-facing", furthermore, my self-confidence had taken a nosedive at that time, and I convinced myself that I didn't have time to go out and not "do work". He insisted and told me about Women in Technology (WIT), so I decided to give it a try. I still remember sitting in my car in the parking lot before the first WIT meeting, terrified. I assumed that these were all technically savvy women who would see through me in a flash. I could not have been more wrong: this first WIT meeting was the beginning of my networking: I joined WIT, was asked to be the chair of the Women Business Group, joined other organizations, went to breakfast meetings, and got to know people and became known. It changed my world in a good way; the complex challenges of the previous year made me stronger and led me in a new direction. This is also the reason I later developed a networking workshop for SCORE: I know how it feels to be terrified of going out after being isolated, and I know the rewards of breaking through this.

I still remember how the VP angrily complained to Dov about what I was doing, but Dov had my back: "She can do whatever she wants to do, and, besides, she's good at this!" I was so grateful to him; soon afterward, the VP resigned.

Some normalcy was restored, but this episode had taken a toll on us. We recognized that, even though the company was profitable and we continued to enjoy working with the team and celebrating the work we were doing, we were getting tired. Very characteristic for this phase, growth was stagnating. We needed a change in strategy to generate renewed excitement and enthusiasm.

Advisory Board

In the early years, we had an advisory board, but we didn't utilize this board very well; it wasn't effective, and it didn't last; it sort of fizzled from a lack of interest and activity. But during the latter part of the growth phase, we decided that an advisory board would be beneficial; I reached out to a group of people in our network with diverse industry expertise and knowledge who could provide advice and a listening ear. It took several months, but we put together a distinguished group of six people. This time I was determined to make this successful, so I had agreements, written expectations, term limits, and the like.

We had quarterly meetings at which we presented our financials, our BD pipeline, and our strategy, and the group would comment, advise, and listen. It was beneficial. After each meeting, we would go for a nice dinner, and we always had a gift for each member.

2010–2012: MATURITY PHASE, GROWTH SLOWDOWN OR NO GROWTH

One day, Paul Leslie, a member of the advisory board, called and asked to speak to me about our Northern Virginia Technology Council (NVTC) membership; as an NVTC committee member, he was tasked with evaluating how small businesses utilized the organization. We met and spoke about NVTC for about 5 minutes or so, then quickly got to Dovel and the BD challenges. He offered to do an evaluation, which showed what we already knew: excellent infrastructure, stalling "growth engine". So, what to do? At the time, Paul was between positions and had time, availability, and interest, so I asked him to be my senior advisor. I gave him complete freedom to talk to anyone in the company, look at records, financials, and so on. The logical conclusion was a change in strategy to avoid decline: continue organic growth efforts and not additional acquisitions. We were in complete agreement! I understood that a drastic shift in strategy required other changes, including leadership, *including me!* I recognized that my strength of organizing, creating a culture, and establishing processes from nothing had served us well during the start-up and growth phases, but a different set of strengths was needed going forward: so we hired Paul to replace me as CEO; such a simple short sentence, but so very loaded . . . more about this in Chapter 9, "Letting Go".

Suffice it to say that we were fortunate, all three of us: for us, Paul was the right person to take Dovel to the next level, and for Paul, Dovel was the perfect opportunity to "do one more deal". Dovel's infrastructure needed updating, for sure, but at the time, it was a strong "platform" company (a company with a foundation that can absorb acquisitions) ready for a strategic change.

Another pivotal moment with great significance happened during Paul's tenure as Dovel's senior advisor: our offices were on the ground floor, and from my office, l looked at the path to the parking lot. Late one morning, Paul, after spending a few hours talking with the staff, stuck his head in my door, told me, "OK, I'm off, see you later", and walked to his car; as I watched him leave, I said to myself: "I need to turn this situation around so that I walk to my car, and Paul sits in my chair". And so it happened!

Before Paul's tenure as CEO, we decided to bid on a large, single-award contract at the FDA; this was a risky move because it was an expensive effort, and we couldn't afford to lose . . . it was an all-or-nothing decision, and we went *all in*. Paul introduced us to a consultant, who, with his team, managed the proposal effort. The same week that Paul started as CEO on Monday, he and Dov delivered the proposal to the FDA on Friday; 6 weeks later, we learned that we had won this single award of a $58 million contract! This was amazing because it provided Paul with the resources to hire the team he wanted, for salaries we had not been able to afford until then, and to fully implement the strategy we agreed on.

2012–2018: RENEWAL OR DEATH

And just like that, we found ourselves in the next phase: renewal or death . . . perhaps a bit dramatic, but at the time, it felt that way.

We made a conscious decision to hire a CEO and give him (almost) free reign; we often hear from founders who want to do what we did, but they do not want to take the risk of hiring someone into the position of CEO; instead, they hire someone as president, or COO and then spend a year looking over this person's shoulder and limiting their ability to implement much-needed change. This usually leads to frustration on both sides, and an unmanageable situation, with the potential CEO leaving and the founder(s) disappointed, exhausted, and back at square one. We concluded that we would be all in, no matter what (more on this in the chapter on risk).

Even though we knew, liked, and trusted Paul, and we knew exactly why we hired him, we were concerned about the different management styles, which involved increased overhead spending on resources we didn't necessarily think we needed or couldn't financially justify. But we stayed the course and continued to support Paul.

This transition of hiring a CEO to replace us is a significant part of our story and something we are often asked about: How did you do it? How did you make it work? Because this is such an important part of the story with multiple angles, we talk about it in several chapters, such as those on scaling the company, letting go, risk tolerance, and more.

During the early part of the renewal phase, the focus was on maturing the team, becoming a recognized brand in the industry, updating our physical space, and updating our procedures and systems.

Several corporate team members were not the right fit for the different leadership style, so a new HR director, a CFO, and an office manager were hired. To his credit, Paul made sure that I met each person before they were hired, which not only made the transition easier for me but I also perceived it as a sign of respect. We retained a director of communications, and press releases went out; this was foreign to us, but *"OK, we're good"*. About a year later, the end of our lease provided an opportunity to significantly upgrade our corporate office space, so a 10-year lease was signed, involving a major (TI-funded) renovation and lots of expensive features. Still, it turned out beautiful, and we stayed within budget. Dov and I did not go with a hammer and nails; there were "people" to do this.

A few months after Paul started, we had an opportunity to acquire a small "company" called ZapThink, whose "product" was thought leadership on cutting-edge technologies that they published in a monthly newsletter. ZapThink had a large and loyal following, and acquiring them gave Dovel visibility and recognition in the industry, one of our objectives. This first acquisition was also a good "dry run" on how acquisitions would go.

Although we submitted bids and won some work in different agencies, substantial organic growth continued to be a challenge; this was exacerbated by situations beyond our control, such as government shutdown and sequestration (2013), and unexpected inability to participate in a contract competition for DTS due to contractual restrictions, as well as those that were in our control, such as poor preparation for bids and internal strive within the team. It came to a situation in which some drastic decisions had to be made for financial reasons, and Paul made them: the salaries of all senior management, including ours, were cut in half for a certain period. It amazed us that all but one team member agreed with this decision and understood the reasons behind it; Dov and I would never have had the courage and confidence to ask our team to make this sacrifice, but we understood that the team perceived it as sound leadership.

We stayed the course of acquisition strategy, and in May 2014, Dovel acquired RN Solution, a business whose main and only contract was the GrantSolutions program at the Department of Health and Human Services; this was a risky acquisition because it was a small business with only one major contract. However, it was also a smart decision because it did not require significant investments, and this acquisition expanded Dovel's footprint in the federal health IT space. In hindsight, and totally to Paul's credit, this acquisition was indeed one of the best decisions. He created a structured deal that involved earn-outs and significant risk mitigation for us.

Overnight, Dovel doubled in size in terms of revenues as well as team size, but it wasn't smooth; there were significant challenges with the integration and management of the GrantSolution contract, and one day, during the summer of 2016, Dov and I got a text message from Paul: "Can we talk". By this time, Dov and I had limited our involvement with the company to board-level oversight, social participation, and trying to attend as many "Friday morning breakfasts" as possible. But this message from Paul got our attention fast, and we talked. He shared with us that, unexpectedly, the PM of the program had rendered his resignation, a blow to the planning, even more so because a major recompete was not far out. So Dov said that he would temporarily function as PM; this had a significant impact on the program positively: he stabilized the program, upgraded the team, and, although the recompete was delayed several times, in the end, Dovel won the recompete. I could have told him about this decision to "temporarily" take on something significant because Dov is still involved at the GrantsSolutions program until today!

Although it took longer than we initially thought, the acquisition strategy was working, and Dovel was growing; definitely, the phase was one of "Renewal" and not "Death". Two years after the RNS acquisition, in May 2016, Dovel acquired Medical Science & Computing, LLC., a company with a headcount and revenues larger than Dovel, with multiple contracts at the National Institutes of Health. This transaction even further enlarged the health-IT footprint of Dovel, making us the largest midsized government health-IT contracting firm. For this transaction, Dovel involved several additional investors, which diluted our equity stake, although we stayed majority owners, and further improved the company's profile as a serious and mature player. The financial stakes were higher, but we had significantly more confidence in Paul and the growth strategy by now.

Increasingly, Dovel's size, financial strength, and footprint in an attractive government market were noticed in the mergers and acquisitions (M&A) world; however, we needed to be 'on the other side' of the GrantsSolutions recompete, a 5-year, $377 million non-small-business set-aside contract that had a significant impact on the valuation of the company. Despite several frustrating delays, the recompete was won in 2018.

As a midsized company with significant revenues (north of $200 million) in desirable government agencies, Dovel was a serious target of interest in the M&A market. We decided that we were not interested in a transaction with a strategic buyer, one in which Dovel would be acquired and absorbed by a larger company whose interest in a deal was due to Dovel's strategic value in the market. Instead, we were looking for a "recapitalization" (recap) transaction: one in which the current equity stakeholders sell their controlling stake of the company to a private equity (PE) firm. The reasons behind this were (a) it would be fairer to our team that, despite the new ownership, the company would continue to exist as Dovel and grow and provide career opportunities, (b) there would not have to be any novation of contracts (consensual replacement of a contract) that would make the conversation with our customers much nicer, and (c) we knew that there was still much potential for Dovel, and with the additional capital, this could be realized. After much interest and many meetings, we, the current stakeholders, sold 90% of our equity to an Australian PE firm in May 2019 and retained 10% in the company. This significant transaction gave the IT government contracting world something to talk about once it hit the presses.

Before beginning the M&A process, we recognized that a succession strategy needed to be in place so that, post-transaction, Paul would not be forced to stay on as CEO for longer than he chooses. So, we interviewed several candidates through a search firm and selected Damon Griggs to join our executive team as COO. His positive outlook and youthful energy made a significant difference in the company. Six months post-transaction, he became the CEO and remained in that position until the final transaction in October 2021.

2019–2021: REVIVAL AND CLOSURE

Let's label the period after the PE transaction the period of revival, even though this began sometime before the transaction. Now, other than board participation for me, we were no longer involved on the corporate level. Dov continued his leadership on the GrantsSolution program, but most people probably did not know who we, the founders, were and what the name Dovel stood for. In September 2019, just a few months after the transaction, Dovel, now controlled by PE, acquired AceInfo, adding footprints in other government agencies and, again, doubling the company size to $400-plus million and 2000-plus FT employees, but Dov and I, as minority equity stakeholders, were not involved in any decision-making. We were enjoying ourselves and watching our company flourish, add valuable solutions to the public, and continue to be a good place for "our" people to work.

In the summer of 2021, Dovel's CEO, Damon, sent us an email, asking if we could talk. He informed us that serious conversations were happening in preparation for a transaction. We were surprised because we had not expected this to happen so fast. A few weeks later, in September 2021, another text from Damon asked us to talk, informing us that the signatures were set and transaction closing was scheduled for October. At the time of this writing, Dovel has been acquired by a company named Guidehouse in a strategic sale. After closing, the company will be absorbed and integrated, the name Dovel will cease to exist, and the signage will come off the buildings in McLean and Rockville! A beautiful ending of a successful journey, 2000 to 2021, from attic to part of a multibillion-dollar enterprise.

Most of the activity of scaling implemented by us, the founders, happened in the *start-up and growth* stages, with us gradually phasing out during the *renewal or death phase*, and finally at observer/investor status during the *revival stage*. We wrote about these scaling activities earlier in this chapter. Still, there were activities during the latter phases that are worth a conversation, as those are no less important to the well-being and thriving of the company and the "ease of mind" of the founders. These activities focused on (a) equity preservation, (b) oversight, (c) supporting the executive team, and (d) culture.

a. **Equity preservation**
    Until Paul joined Dovel, we were the only equity holders; however, this changed with Paul, and soon, to a lesser extent, another senior executive. Dov and I determined that, together, we would hold more than 50.1% or less than 10% of the equity. The reasoning was about control: if we held majority equity, we retained control, but when the time came to give up a controlling stake, we did not want to have a personal asset of significant value without controlling it. Over the next few years, as part of acquisitions, additional investors were added, but Dov and I always retained at least 50.1% ownership. We implemented a plan to reward our team for their valuable input and to show recognition that we would not have been successful without them. The Equity Bonus Plan is described in more detail in Chapter 10, "Preparing for Exit".

b. **Oversight**
    Bringing in a third party in the role of CEO was a significant change for us. Dov and I were the only equity holders with no other stakeholders to consider or consult until then. There was no need for executive oversight, but with someone else as the CEO, a title and position that comes with significant decision powers, this changed. Scaling at this junction involved "flexible" oversight; there was a considerable measure of trust and respect between Paul and us, but we still wanted to ensure that we were kept informed and that certain decisions were made, if not by us, then at least with us. What we wanted to avoid at all costs is a situation in which Paul had to ask us too frequently for permission or, on the other hand, that changes were made that would put our company at too significant a risk. We learned of many situations that had not worked out well because the owners were too restrictive with the CEO. We wanted to avoid that; we wanted to ensure that

this partnership was successful, and we recognized that this was on us as much as it was on Paul.

When we handed the CEO role to him, our board was the three of us. So, instead of telling Paul to ask us for permission, we wrote in the bylaws that certain decisions required board consent; these were actions such as increasing the LOC or securing a bank loan; changing legal, banking, or accounting relationships, and hiring executive-level resources. Over time, it became clear that these bylaws were unnecessary: the three of us developed a habit of meeting after the Friday morning breakfast and talking about what was going on in the company and with the team. Paul was also very mindful and respectful of us, as we were respectful of him. We are very proud of our successful partnership, in which each of us had different strengths and in which all of us recognized the value that each of us brought to the team.

c. **Supporting the CEO**
    Elma: Our team was used to us and loyal to us, so when Paul came in as CEO, we needed to show our support and confidence in him. We called an all-hands meeting, and I gave a speech about Paul joining us and the reasons behind this decision: I wrote my words because I wanted to make sure to get it right, and I also didn't want to get emotional. It wasn't just me who got a little emotional; others came up later to hug me in appreciation. During the first few months, people sometimes came to me with concerns or questions. I would immediately refer them to Paul; we never questioned or criticized his decisions behind his back, and we made sure to show support and confidence. This is not to say that we didn't ask him behind closed doors from time to time.

    One time, our HR director and I met for lunch, at her request; I told Paul ahead of time, and, sensing his concern, I assured him that I would never criticize or question him, so not to worry about that. Pretty soon, these encounters no longer occurred.

    Dov and I wanted to make sure that Paul had all the tools needed to succeed; after all, his success was our success! This included financial resources: the $58 million win was helpful but not enough, so we agreed to keep our salaries relatively modest (the three of us were certainly not the highest paid) and to forgo all earnings distributions; as an S-Corp, the corporate taxes were paid at the shareholders' level, so tax distributions were made. Again, when we share this with founders who want to "do what we did", they look shocked because they do not want to take that kind of financial risk. But we were all in and determined to make the partnership with Paul work.

d. **Culture**

From the beginning, the company's culture was essential to us. That didn't end with the leadership change; Dov was usually at the GrantsSolution program, which was in Rockville, Maryland, while the corporate team was in McLean, Virginia. I did my best to attend as many Friday-morning breakfasts as possible and include everyone in a conversation. Dov attended when he could, and Paul was always at the table. I know that this was received well by the team. In addition, Dov and I, avid hikers, encouraged people to come hiking with us; another team manager took on the responsibility to organize hikes, which were often full-day events. Dov and I always participated, and we loved it; I wished there would have been more hikes with larger teams, but regardless, it was fun. We posted pictures and socialized the Hiking Club. Also, the CAPS tickets were a hit and a big part of our team culture. We often came to a game not knowing the people who sat with us, other Dovel employees . . . it was a great way to introduce ourselves. After the 2019 transaction, our roles were diminished, and we could no longer keep team activities going. However, the Dovel culture is still something that people talk about, and we're very proud of that.

Summary

This was a very long chapter with a lot of information; writing this was a trip down memory lane, some good, some not so great. We would love to say that we were masters at this and that we have much to teach, but the truth is that we can share because we made mistakes, we got some of it right, some of it wrong, and much of it we know only in hindsight.

To the founder(s), we say this:

Scaling is about systems and organizational structures as well as about you as leaders. Know your strengths and work with them; then recognize when different leadership strengths are needed and adjust. This is scaling, and it worked for us all the way!

4

BAGELS ON FRIDAYS

We are firm believers in developing <u>and maintaining</u> relationships.

Dovel was built on the relationships that were developed and maintained throughout our personal lives and professional careers.

Whether Holiday parties at our house when Dovel was small, where to Dov's amazement, Elma called every employee, spouse, and child by name, to corporate group activities in which they participated as much as possible, Dov and Elma's objective was always to know everyone.

Towards the end of the company's life cycle it was clear that this culture of inclusion and connection was impactful to the team, and a reason for them to consider Dovel a good place to work.

In this chapter you will read how relationships led to contractual opportunities, established a corporate culture still valued until today, and resulted in the impactful change in growth strategy with a new CEO.

Also in this chapter, Elma provides key points from her half-day workshop, "Networking 101". She reminds people that the benefits of networking are not always immediate, and that Networking is not about scoring a sale.

We hope this chapter will inspire entrepreneurs to develop business relationships and networking skills, in person as well as on social media.

DOI: 10.4324/9781003260653-6

BAGELS ON FRIDAYS   61

Elma

If there is one theme that permeates throughout our story, personal and professional, it's "relationships". It's the glue that binds people and the foundation for opportunities, career advancements, friendships, and more. Recognizing this at an intuitive level, we made it part of our unspoken strategy when building Dovel and developing the culture we wanted.

Relationships played a role in how we came to be in the U.S.: we were invited to stay with friends of Dov's parents; they maintained a relationship, despite the distance and the lack of the tools we now take for granted, like Skype and so on, so when Dov needed a place to stay in Washington, D.C., the "ask" to them was easy because the relationship was maintained. Other friends in Washington, D.C. walked over to George Washington University to ensure that Dov's application and other documents were received; again, not an uncomfortable "ask" because the relationship was there already.

Looking back at the importance of *relationships* in the Dovel success, several stories illustrate the impact (I will get to the bagels, I promise).

Dov got his major professional break because he had maintained his relationship with his previous boss. In addition to them working together, we socialized: went on hikes, weekend trips, and other events. So when this ex-boss was asked for "the best IT architect he ever met" for a recently won large government contract, he mentioned Dov . . . and that's how the first major government contracting engagement, EDGAR, happened.

Fast-forward, other engagements were added, and we establish Integrated Data Corporation (IDC; later Dovel). One of the subcontractors to IDC/Dovel employed a team of a few dozen people at the program on which we filled multiple leading positions. I made it part of my role to regularly go to the work site and walk around to talk to "our" team as well as to the second-tier people who worked for us; I got to know them, and as they began to know and trust me, they shared their concerns and challenges. At holiday time, we left a personal card with a $25 gift card on each person's desk. This team felt ignored by their direct employer, but they felt listened to and loyal to us, Dov and Elma. As a result, when one of the team members had an opportunity to join the FDA, he reached out to us, and we established the contract with the FDA and provided a path for him to be in the position. This was a direct result of the effort of building and maintaining relationships with this team. Through this relationship at the FDA, we learned of other project opportunities for IDC/Dovel; we submitted proposals, beat the competition, and won: our first two prime contracts were at the FDA!

Now for the bagels.

We started out in an attic, graduated to "shared office" space, and ultimately had to make the scary jump to leased space. We signed a lease in an office building in Tysons Corner, one half of the ground floor, and rapidly outgrew the space. So, we added the space on the other side. This resulted in two kitchens, two conference rooms, and two "water coolers", which rapidly became an impediment to creating a cohesive team. One of our employees had taken on the responsibility of bringing in a bag of fresh bagels on Friday mornings, which was great! He would put the bag in alternating kitchens, so no one felt left out. Several weeks went by, until one Friday morning when I noticed how people would come into the kitchen, prepare their bagel, and run back to their desk to eat it. This completely missed the intent of spending some time together as a team and socializing. I had learned about the importance of sitting and eating together as a team during a work break when I worked in Meir Hospital in Kfar Saba, Israel. Eating and talking are two major pastimes in Israel, so every morning, 10 a.m., a long table was set, filled with breakfast food, and everyone – doctors, nurses, techs, and so on – would sit together and eat/talk for about 30 minutes. What a wonderful concept and an amazing way to build cohesion and team culture. So, in that moment, I said to an employee who happened to be in the kitchen with me: "No more of this, from now on we are going to have breakfast 'the European Way', with tablecloths on the tables". He was stunned, started laughing, and helped me arrange the tables in, what we called, the training room. It took a few weeks to really get this going, I had to convince senior management to come and sit; we added additional items to the breakfast, fruit, sweets, and more; over time we added a toaster and, much later, waffles, bacon, and eggs were "made to order". This "Bagels on Fridays" became, and is until today, something that is done every Friday morning, our recruiters mention it to potential new hires as an illustration of Dovel's culture, and often they are invited to come and sit with us. The conversations are about sharing stories, and not about work, politics, religion, and so on. It is where the newly hired administrative assistant sits together with the CEO, a senior manager, or the founder and has a friendly personal interaction. The impact may not be immediately visible, but the team feels and respects the climate of inclusion and acceptance and appreciates being listened to. Multiple times I heard from people outside the company "we heard about the bagels on Friday at Dovel" as a compliment.

Finally, a long-standing professional–personal relationship provided Dov and me with the opportunity to implement a strategy of acquisition when organic growth slowed down. I had put together a well-respected advisory board of about six to seven people, all seasoned executives in the industry; we had maintained long-term relationships with each of them, with mutual respect and trust. It was a one-on-one conversation with one member, Paul Leslie, that led to him joining Dovel as a senior advisor, and after a few months, as CEO. Paul was instrumental in implementing the strategy of acquisition, which caused Dovel to grow rapidly, and it was Paul's network of relationships in the private equity (PE) world that ultimately led to the sale of our equity to PE. The fact that we had a long-standing trusting relationship of mutual respect meant that Dov and I had complete confidence in Paul's integrity and capabilities and that we were able to work well together for several years until May 2019, the month of the transaction. Until this day we meet socially and have great respect for each other.

Each story is different, as each relationship is different; what they all have in common is the following.

1. Relationships Take Time, Commitment, and Effort to Develop

In the networking workshop I created, and presented quarterly, as a mentor for SCORE I emphasize a few key points that I want to share with you. Participants of the workshop typically voice similar challenges: time, a lack of discipline toward commitment, and confidence.

For my coaching practice, I developed a tool to support clients with achieving objectives and goals; this tool is now widely used by SCORE mentors as they work with clients, and I see how clients find it very helpful. Here it is.

See how simple this really is? You set your own SMART (specific, measurable, attainable, relevant, time-based) goals, create a strategy that works for you, mitigate the challenges that you already know of and that can torpedo your success, and then visualize

Table 4.1 The Tool to Achieving Objectives and Goals

Objective	Goal	Strategy	Challenge	Mitigation	Vision
Develop relationships	By December 31, I will have 3 new contacts with whom I am in touch at least monthly and whom I feel comfortable asking for a favor.	Attend events. Join a club Invite someone to meet for coffee.	No time Too timid	Schedule, put on your calendar, and go! Commit to attend. The Thinking Path	Visualize what it looks like/ feels like, to have a wider circle of comfortable relationships to draw on

reaching your objective. I advise that you write these down, on a whiteboard, or on a pad that you see every day; some of you might need to be held accountable, so ask a friend, a coach, or a partner to sit with you on a regular basis and go over it. No beating yourself up, however, if you did not meet your goal; just ask yourself if your goal wasn't SMART or perhaps your strategy needs adjusting.

So this tool supports you with time and commitment. What about confidence?

Enter **The Thinking Path**, . . . a very simple mindset that goes like this:

How you think determines how you feel, which determines your actions which determines results.

Example: Friday morning breakfast at Dovel . . .

Thoughts: having a conversation with senior people in the company is so scary, what if I say something stupid, what if they ask me something. . .
Feelings: intimidated, nervous, shy, uncomfortable
Action: take a bagel and eat it at your desk
Result: no connections are made, no new relationships can develop

or

Thoughts: wow, what a great opportunity to meet people in the company
Feelings: excited, confident, ready for action. . .
Action: introducing yourself, joining the table for Friday bagels, joining a conversation. . .
Result: connections made, new relationship can develop

The interesting thing about this is that you control it, it's your mindset.

2. *The Benefit Is Not Immediately Visible*

Relationships take time to develop, and your objective should not be to "score a sale" in the first conversation. A real relationship is one of trust, empathy, and sharing, and the way for that to develop is to ask open-ended questions: What do they like about. . . ? How did they arrive. . . ? What are your challenges with. . . ? People ask me, "When is a good time to give my elevator speech, or to talk about what I need (my 'ask')?" I tell them, "Learn about the other person first, what makes them happy, sad . . . learn how can you be of value to the other before you worry about how the other can be useful to you".

As illustrated in the example stories earlier in the chapter, it usually isn't immediately clear what the specific benefits of a certain relationship will be, but one thing is clear . . . building and maintaining relationships is a key factor of success, and facilitating relationship building in your organization is sure to enhance the culture and working environment.

3. *Not Every Relationship Works Out*

Now, having said all that, here's the other side of relationship building we've learned: not every relationship works out. Despite all the wonderful experiences, and amazing people we've met and connected with over the years, Dov and I have often said that if there's one thing we wish we didn't have to learn, it is about how toxic and underhanded some people can be. There have been times when we hired people or did business with people only to learn that our values did not align or that their agendas were not constructive for us and the company or they were just "negative energy". We recognized the true nature of these toxic people often too late, and damage was done. Looking back, I realize that, almost every time, I knew deep inside that these were relationships best avoiding, but I either didn't trust my own instinct, or there were other, seemingly more beneficial, benefits to the relationship, and I waved away the "red flags". With the great benefit of hindsight, my advice to you is to *listen to your "inner voice"*; trust your instincts and avoid relationships with people who just don't "feel right"; it will save you a lot of pain and worries.

5

SHOULD MARRIED COUPLES RUN A BUSINESS TOGETHER?

We get this question all the time, so we are devoting and entire chapter to this.

We are married partner for 40 years, and business partner for more than half that time. When the question comes up, as it does frequently, *"if you knew then what you know now, would you do the business partnership again?"*

Dov answers, "Oh, absolutely, for sure"

Elma answers, "Well, let's talk; you may want to think about it"

Family businesses have unique challenges. Statistics and our observations show that the failure rate is high among husband-and-wife business partnerships because of the additional strain on the relationship.

Our Guiding Principles involve swim-lanes and ground rules around The Three Rs.

Readers will gain insight into how we successfully combined marriage and business by recognizing the complementary qualities and strengths we each bring to the table. You will also learn about personality differences and the challenges we overcame as we built Dovel together.

While we don't claim to have the answer on this, this chapter might provide readers with ideas and in-sights on developing guiding principles and ground-rules for partnerships in business and life.

DOI: 10.4324/9781003260653-7

We get asked this question a lot, especially as we speak to students at universities: they hear our story and want to be like us: "I can be like Dov, and my wife can be like Elma"; it's not that simple, you hear what you want to hear, and you see what you want to see. You hear us speak at the end of a journey that never had a guaranteed outcome, and you don't see the challenges, risks, and sleepless nights. There were many uncertainties, close calls, and risky decisions that could have led to a different outcome, for both the company and us as a couple.

Dov

Challenges of a Business and Marriage Partnership

The start-up phase can be exciting, but it also presents challenges. In these early days, it was beneficial for both of us to have a business partner whom we could rely on and who we could fully trust. From the beginning, we developed "swim lanes" so that we each had our domain: I owned technical and customer relationships, and Elma owned corporate governance. She felt strongly, in a negative way, about the term *back office*, and I quickly learned never to use that term. It wasn't always simple, however, as business challenges have a way of seeping into the personal relationship and family dynamics. As married partners and as parents, we both knew that we should leave the business in the office and switch to marriage/family matters at home, but as business owners, this proved to be a challenge, even more so when the corporate offices were in our home.

We established rules to avoid conflict: no business talk at the dinner table; Elma made sure that we had dinner (and breakfast for that matter) together with Mark and Karyn at the kitchen table every day, but there were days when we both experienced challenges from our domain, and some of it overlapped. Besides, we were often tired and overwhelmed, which caused tempers to be a little short.

As the company grew and senior managers were added to the team, the problems grew. Nobody ever challenged or questioned me, mainly because I was the main information technology (IT) expert at Dovel, but it was also obvious to me that my gender played a major role in this. The government IT contracting world is a male-dominated industry, and for Elma, the trifecta of being female, my wife, and not technical was incredibly challenging. It was often difficult for me to hear some of the comments and not lash out. The difference in how each one of us was treated by, and therefore had to deal with, some of the senior managers put a strain on our relationship as well. The business partnership was impacting our marriage relationship and not in a good way.

Even though this problem was not true with most staff, in a small company, it doesn't take much for someone to create trouble; there were a few individuals who caused such toxicity that it caused us to almost lose it all, our business as well as our marriage partnership. Fortunately, we got through it; we managed to remove both executives.

Looking back, we recognized the risk of allowing outsiders to deliberately create a wedge with the objective of gaining influence, and it never happened again. We learned from it and became stronger because of it. Also, we learned about the challenge of adding senior members into a small cohesive team and the damage that can be caused by a "bad hire"; obviously, a growing company involves expanding the team, but our bad experience caused us to be much more cautious.

Until today, despite our success and the many wonderful experiences, that part of our story creates unpleasant and painful memories, both to us as business partners as well as to us as marriage partners.

So back to the question of whether married couples should go in business together. The strength and resiliency of the existing relationship matter, as does the ability to evolve and grow together, be honest with each other, and agree on the purpose and end game of the business. We didn't set out to build a company that, 20 years later, would sell to a private equity firm in a major transaction, but we agreed on adjusting strategy whenever this was required for the success of the business. This requires trust and similar levels of risk tolerance.

I urge you not to take our story as an example that it will always work out because in most cases (approximately 75%) it does not. The combined pressures of marriage, parenting, and business cause many couples to call it quits; however, leaving one partnership without damaging or leaving the other is almost impossible as, over time, a symbiotic connection has developed.

Will you be honest enough with each other and have these conversations before events cause irreparable damage? Will you recognize the danger in time to avoid damage? Only you and your partner can know the answer to this.

As for us, I am proud to say that we successfully navigated the pressures with respect to the business, as well as the marriage, partnership. I can honestly say that, despite the challenges, pain, and hard work, the reward of building a successful business together and coming out of this adventure stronger and more resilient made it all worthwhile.

Elma

We want to be like you and Dov; how did you do it?

We hear this often because young entrepreneurial couples look at our success and want to "be like us". "It's easy, right? I will be like Dov, and my wife will do the back office like you". My part of this chapter is about that one sentence.

First, it's obviously not easy and not without tremendous risk; in their eagerness to see possibilities, people often speed right by the most important aspects; you are not Dov, your wife is not me, your relationship is not like ours, nor is your risk tolerance, your flexibility, your financial situation, and so on; I could go on, but you get the point. Take a hard look at your relationship and have an honest and objective evaluation of its strengths and challenges. Adding a business relationship to any personal relationship can create a dynamic wrought with strife but adding it to a marital relationship really "rocks the boat". So that's why my response is "Let's talk about this".

Second, how to decide on roles and responsibilities (or, as we call it, swim lanes) in a business partnership isn't as easy as one person deciding who does what and the other person complying; the key is to clearly recognize strengths and skills, preferences and "best fits". The strengths must be complementary, and not competing. For Dov and me, the roles were clear, based on an honest look at our strengths and skills. It is important that this is decided together by both partners and *by design, not by default* (I use this line a lot because it creates focus and forces conversations).

Finally, for this to be a true and equal partnership, there must be respect for the role each partner takes on. One of our first conversations on adding business partnership to marriage partnership centered on my concerns about becoming "the wife in the back office"; I banned the term *back office* from our vocabulary and labeled my "swim lane" corporate governance, which Wikipedia defines as

> provid[ing] the framework for attaining a company's objectives, it encompasses practically every management sphere, from action plans and internal controls to performance measurement and corporate disclosures.[1]

So it appears that we had it all figured out from the get-go, right? If only that were true. In the remainder of this chapter, I discuss three concepts as they pertain to the business/marriage relationship:

- relationship,
- roles and responsibilities, and
- respect,

along with how I recognized the importance of each in hindsight and how we got it wrong multiple times and still succeeded.

Relationship

I remember our first conversation about starting a business partnership very clearly, I even remember where we were (on the street walking our dog, Maggy) and what month it was (January 2000). I vehemently rejected the idea! You should know that, as a Dutch woman, I usually have very strong opinions about most things. At that time, Dov had the early beginnings of a business, with a team consisting of all subcontractors on one subcontract but no infrastructure or corporate systems. I had taken on some support level tasks but was not interested in a true business partnership because I was convinced that "husband and wife should not work together!" and I avoided any conversation about it until that time. Somehow, this time was different because there were other considerations: (a) I was between jobs and interviewing for an academic health care position that I was excited about, (b) we bought an old house that needed renovation and our current home was on the market, and (c) Dov had the opportunity to gain a large contract, the Defense Travel System (DTS) which required multiple security cleared personnel. There was an intersection between necessity, opportunity, and timing. After careful consideration, I decided to take it on for 6 months: renovate a house, sell our house, set up a corporate infrastructure, and keep our family sane and organized. . . *yeah, I can do that!* "But", I clearly recall saying to Dov, "if it gets in the way of our relationship, we'll stop it". I learned over the years that it's not that simple because situations come up, other people influence the dynamic, and patterns develop. Walking away is not an option that can be chosen easily.

A few examples:

Sometime during the second year, there was an opportunity to develop a strategic business teaming relationship with a large commercial company; at the time, we still had only one (sub)contract; all employees were billable on the one subcontract, except for a 1.5 full-time equivalent for office support; and corporate HQ was still in our attic. For this business opportunity to develop we needed someone to work it, so we hired someone who had been an executive for a small start-up and who, we believed, had the skills and personality to make this work; besides, he was available and open to be compensated on a consulting month-to-month contractual basis. All good, except it became clear fast that he did not consider me worthy to speak to; he spoke only to Dov. I recognized this as a combination of misogyny and arrogance, and I tried to work it by employing fake deference and strong professional language but to no avail. I didn't want to lose the business opportunity and blamed myself for this bad dynamic, but Dov had my back. Pretty soon, we recognized that he wasn't going to develop anything and that it wouldn't be such a problem if he walked, so I put forward an ultimatum that resulted in his resignation. What I remember most of this episode is that Dov stood with me, a true partnership.

Another example took longer to resolve and was more painful for both of us. About 7 or 8 years into the Dovel journey, we recognized that we needed additional senior leadership; by then, we were in our corporate offices in Tysons Corner, Dovel had multiple programs, prime and sub, at multiple agencies, and the company was at the stage of advanced rapid growth. We interviewed multiple candidates and decided on one with experience growing a small company, the perfect candidate who presented well. About 2 to 3 months into his tenure, the problems began: twisting facts, telling lies about me to Dov and other senior leaders, and creating an overall toxic dynamic. I was vulnerable because in general, I believed that I must be the one who moderates relationships, gets along with everyone, and is responsible for a positive team culture; also, I had just lost my father which added to the overall emotional exhaustion and vulnerability. At that time, Dov was very busy with multiple contracts and didn't have the time or mental energy to deal with any of it. It became a very difficult time for us, both professionally and personally, and several times I considered walking away. However, as I alluded to earlier in this chapter, it's not that simple, during the rapid growth phase of the company, there aren't enough senior leaders in corporate governance to keep it going, and besides, this is the key challenge, the business and marriage partnerships are now intertwined . . . one does not survive without the other. So, what to do: firing him was not an option because, through lies and manipulation, he had built himself a fiefdom in the company, and my efforts to improve the professional relationship with him had backfired several times as he considered this a sign of weakness and used it to his advantage. I decided that I needed to be strong, continue running the business, be a role model to my team, and muscle through it. I was convinced that this situation would resolve itself one way or another, and it did when Dov began to see the manipulation and deceit, agreed to put up boundaries that quickly resulted in resignation and departure. We both look back at these 14 months as the most difficult time of our personal and professional relationship.

Here is the silver lining, however.

First, I developed a mindset that continued to be useful for years: I told myself that I would not allow *THIS* (meaning business partnership–related problems) to ruin our marriage because *THIS* is always temporary; it became my mantra, and it worked for me. My friends and anyone else who wants to hear (not my kids, they roll their eyes) know what I consider nonnegotiable marriage destroyers: the three As: abuse, adultery, and addiction (the last one with some consideration, of course), and business partnership problems is not one of those.

Second, there is a lot of truth to the old saying: *That what doesn't kill you makes you stronger*; working through and overcoming this challenge made me and *us* stronger.

And finally, although initially my self-confidence took a nosedive, I came back stronger and more confident; I recognized that I needed to get out of the office more, attend networking events, show the industry who I was at Dovel, and become "the face of Dovel". Dov supported me and was very proud of seeing me in this new role.

So, when considering a business/marriage partnership, accept the fact that you are adding challenges that nonbusiness partners don't have. Commit to have each other's back, determine for yourself what are nonnegotiable marriage breakers, and, in the end, look at what you've gained and not what you've lost.

Roles and Responsibilities

A start-up, especially in the early stages, typically doesn't have separate departments for the various corporate and operational functions, and there are no clearly defined roles and responsibilities. It's very much: everyone does whatever needs to be done to keep things rolling and bring in revenues. As soon as there is more than one person in a leadership position, it becomes key to define "work ownership" and responsibility; we used to call this "swim lanes". The metaphor to swim lanes works because we're in the same pool (company), which has parallel lanes (areas of responsibility) of identical lengths and depth (one lane is not more important or challenging than the other); we have the same objective (to win), and we swim in the same direction.

In determining who does what in the organization, it is critical to evaluate each person's strengths, skills, and experience; in our case, it was clear that Dov had the technical background and the operational leadership skills to "own" the responsibility for the direct (meaning billable) work, whereas my strengths are organization, communication, and multitasking, all skills that were developed and strengthened during my years as a health care provider.

Once we both understood, and agreed with, the "division" of labor on the leadership level, it became easier to develop and scale our roles without getting into each other's "swim lane" and causing confusion or friction. This also facilitated our conversations and decision-making and mitigated the potential for conflict about "ownership of work".

Finally, one swim lane is not more important than the other!

A solid corporate infrastructure enables the billable labor to create value for the customer, and high quality, high-value billable work brings in revenues for the company to grow . . . and ultimately, that's the objective.

Respect

Just as we understand that one swim lane (area of work) is not more important than the other; likewise, one person's role is not more important than the other, and nowhere is this more important to keep in mind than in the business/married partnership; a lack of respect or failure to recognize value quickly erodes the enthusiasm of even the most well-meaning husband–wife business partnerships.

This is especially important when interfacing with third parties, that is, lawyers, accountants, and so on. It was very common, in meetings where Dov and I both attended, for people to direct their questions to Dov, regardless of the subject matter. And usually, it wasn't just the questions, but the body language and focus of the conversation were to Dov. To his credit, Dov would frequently set the record straight by answering, "*Contracts, (or accounting, HR, etc.)?* You need to ask Elma, because that is not in my area of expertise". Confusion and big eyes would show, after which the conversation would begin to include me. I must admit I resented being the "potted plant" in the room and sometimes compensated by interrupting or speaking louder, but I was always grateful for the respect Dov showed me in front of others; he was not afraid to be perceived as weak for showing his respect for me and my role in the company.

In Summary

There is no easy answer to the question, "Should married partners become business partners?" and we certainly do not have the answers, nor did we always get it right. I hope that this chapter has provided some material for contemplation and conversation before you dive in.

Make sure that your decision is by design and not by default, and that you have talked about the critical elements: relationships, roles and responsibilities, and respect.

However, for sure, it would have been significantly more complicated should both of us have been technical or nontechnical and naturally, we would gravitate into the same swim lane, so to speak, and would bump into each other daily. So, please give it some thought before you jump into it.

Note

1   https://en.wikipedia.org/wiki/Corporate_governance, accessed January 10, 2022.

6

DOV'S TECH TALES – THE ONLY CONSTANT IS CHANGE

This chapter is pure tech written for tech entrepreneurs, engineers, and everyone who loves talking technology and is interested in reading about tech and its history. Dov has led the full life-cycle software development and technical architecture of large mission-critical government information technology (IT) systems for three decades and is taking the time to bring these efforts to life. All the way from the Electronic Data Gathering and Retrieval (EDGAR) system built for the Securities and Exchange Commission (SEC) and to GrantSolutions.gov, where he is still involved as a senior advisor.

DOI: 10.4324/9781003260653-8

Dov

Everyone who knows me knows that, at my core, I am a techie.

As the rate of change of technologies accelerated over the past few decades, and from the very first day of Integrated Data Corporation (IDC), we adopted an environment of continuous learning, and we encouraged employees to continue adapting and exploring new ways and new technologies. This has become a Dovel guiding principle until this very day.

Online Trademark Research System

When, in the early days of IDC, opportunity knocked on my door, and I was asked to build a trademark research system for Compu-Mark that would allow companies to perform online research of trademarks – I said yes. Keep in mind that, at the time, all trademark research was done by sending people into the Patent and Trademark Office (USPTO) to conduct a manual search – a difficult, expensive, and time-consuming process. To get the trademark database, CompuMark and the USPTO agreed to automate the paper-based database by having CompuMark automate, give one electronic copy to the USPTO and keep one copy. This was the copy that CompuMark would use in the Online Trademark Research System.

I brought in two George Washington University (GWU) students, whom I had connected with during my studies, and we built a system that was ahead of its time. The first phase was to implement a system that allowed the CompuMark in-house staff to conduct online searches. The objective of the second phase was to allow a person outside of CompuMark but in the D.C. area to connect to our system using a PC and conduct a trademark search.

When a string of characters was entered, our system would present back entries from our database that looked, or sounded, similar, in which case there would be a conflict that prevented the person from successfully registering the proposed trademark.

We used some technologies that we "played" with at GWU and we had a system that allowed people to dial up (remember those days? 300-, 1200-, 9600-baud modems connecting over telephone lines?) and do online what they previously had to do by calling a research person in CompuMark's office.

The system was a success, and it allowed many trademark researchers to conduct multiple searches and explore the viability of their potential trademark. Later, CompuMark was acquired by an international entity, and the Online Trademark Research System, built by us, a few young students, became part of something much larger. This was in the early 1990s: my first experience building a large system.

EDGAR

Filing Automation, EDGARLink, and Standard Generalized Markup Language

In 1989, BDM International won the contract to develop the ED-GAR system, and I received a call from my friend, Tom Woteki, who was the technical lead on the EDGAR team at BDM. I joined the BDM team as a subcontractor to design and implement the very first online filing system for the SEC. Over the years, I have met many people who were surprised to hear that I was the one behind some of the technologies used in this system. One of the areas my team was responsible for was the EDGARLink filing software. Now go back to these years, early 1990: no internet, no large government electronic filing systems, no electronic scanning of hundreds of pages of government forms and electronic analysis of data in these documents in a timely way filing deadlines, and no good way to transmit these large filings. The team I was heading was ready to tackle these (and many more) issues.

We looked at these massive filings and computed how long it would take companies to upload these documents using a 300B modem; 9600B modem came a few years later and wasn't common for many smaller companies that were mandated to report to the

SEC. The unlikely chance that the upload would complete successfully convinced me that we needed to implement a restart capability. What this involved was that the PC would keep track of where the upload was in the process, and if anything were to disrupt the data flow, the PC would remember that position; then, when EDGARLink was started, it would recognize that it's a restart scenario and automatically, without human interaction, resume the upload. Easier said than done, and revolutionary at the time

The world of open-source software didn't exist as it does today, but we found the source code for X modem[1] and later for Z modem,[2] and since most companies file a very large annual report (10-K) on the last business day of March between 3:00 p.m. and 5:00 p.m., we concluded that any interruption of the upload session and a restart from the beginning will prevent most filers from completing the transmission by 5:00 p.m. Therefore, we decided that we must design and implement a restart capability whereby the transmission will resume only from where it stopped when transmission was interrupted. Thus, the EDGARLink restart came to being and served the filer community for many years – a very advanced capability in those days.

The EDGAR system was being integrated into an existing, fully operational system that supported growing volumes of data, and part of the process was to increasingly mandate companies to use the system. In those early days, the office of EDGAR management held extensive semiannual meetings with filers at the SEC. Hundreds of people showed up, including the press, and we briefed our progress and our plans. Before one of these meetings, when the EDGARLink restart was ready for prime time, I suggested we demo it by starting an upload, yanking the PC power cord from the outlet, and plugging it back in. If all worked well, the PC would recognize the EDGARLink restart mode, automatically dial the EDGAR system and resume the filing from where it was interrupted. We all agreed that this would be a high-risk, high-reward, and worthwhile demo and that it was time to show the capability in real time.

At the subsequent filers' meeting, we put a PC on the stage, started the demo, and before we managed to yank the power cable, the entire D.C. area lost power! Clearly, unanticipated. We began exploring what happened while attempting to entertain the few hundred people waiting in the room.

We used to do "timing tests" to determine the time it would take after a power start-up for the system to reboot, start dialing, and begin transmitting from where it left off. But I had a simpler test: when we yanked the power, a sweat bead will develop in my neck, and travel down my back. If the sweat bead arrived at my pants, something was very wrong – it was taking too long.

When the power came back, like clockwork, the "Dov timing test" started. The sweat bead started traveling as the PC rebooted, I felt it around my middle spine as the PC went into a restart mode and down my waist as it initiated the dialup connection and resumed transmission. The sweat bead didn't make below my belt. When the transmission demo was completed, the crowd clapped, and our team had lost a few pounds.

Another story I remember vividly was the implementation of the EDGAR formatter/parser. EDGAR had close to 300 types of filings in those days. Some are very well known, such as 10-K and 10Q, and some are more esoteric and not known to most people. Each of the forms had many data elements that were tagged so that the system could recognize the piece of information and load it into the database. We selected the Standard Generalized Markup Language (SGML[3]) tagging scheme. HTML is based on SGML. We found an open-source parser, but we had to write a significant amount of code to enable it to handle the breadth and depth of many EDGAR filings, and the implementation was running into difficulties and behind schedule.

One day, Tom asked me to join him to a Baltimore Orioles baseball game (no Washington Nationals in early 1990.) As a foreigner, I knew nothing about baseball, but I agreed to join Tom. On the way from D.C. to Baltimore, I heard the main reason behind the invitation: Tom asked me, "Hey, Dov, what do you think if you and I take over programming the formatter/parser?" Since the formatter/parser wasn't part of my team's responsibility I didn't have all the details, but I knew that two of the top managers can't just like that become full-time programmers and ignore their management responsibilities; who would lead the project and manage a large team under very tight deadlines and with many different and shifting challenges? So I told Tom that I did not think it was a good idea but that I could spend more time looking into it.

We walked into the baseball stadium, and I was in awe of the size and the beauty. Tom, an avid baseball fan, explained to me the baseball rules. He then proceeded to unfold his newspaper, sip his beer, and eat his hotdog, occasionally watching the game . . . what an all-American experience.

The issues with the formatter/parser kept us busy for a long time, but we managed to get it to do what it needed to do at acceptable performance levels in time for the first production release. One day we got a message from the director of the office of EDGAR management: "Congressional subcommittee on oversight and investigation is concerned about the security risk imbedded in the EDGAR system". We attempted to have a meaningful dialog about the security of the EDGAR system, but we were not making good progress. It was clear that there was a political agenda behind this conversation, slowing down the rollout of EDGAR or, worse shutting it down altogether. At a moment of frustration, we suggested to the director of the office of EDGAR management, "How about we give them three days to penetrate the system, if they are successful, we can address the issues they found, if they are not, they will have to go away". Luckily, we had a very good relationship with this director, and he communicated our suggestion to the oversight committee in Congress. For 3 days, their security gurus attempted to break into the system, unsuccessfully; we never heard their concerns about EDGAR system vulnerabilities again. On July 16, 1992, the EDGAR system went operational, an amazing accomplishment for the entire EDGAR/BDM team, and a major leap forward in convenience to the public.

Since the days of the EDGAR system, there have been significant changes in the IT landscape. It's nowadays unthinkable to have to transmit a few hundred pages of SEC filing over a 300B modem. It evolved to where we no longer think in these terms with to-day's internet speed. Who would have expected in early 1990 that, 25 years later, we will be able to stream anything over the internet without any issues? It took a bit of time, but the vision that was laid down in the early days is now in place.

American Red Cross

Blood Distribution System

In early 2000, the American Red Cross (ARC) managed multiple computer systems nationwide, each serving one or more regions. The Food and Drug Administration (FDA) inspected these systems and identified shortcomings, so in 2003, they issued a consent de-cree requiring the ARC to address them. As the prime contractor for this program, BDM recommended consolidating the multiple systems. IDC/Dovel was a main subcontractor to BDM for this program, and I was the technical architect. We selected and en-hanced a system to accommodate the mission of this organization: the collection, testing, and distribution of over 50% of the na-tion's blood supply. We established a nationwide network and, as this system was considered a "medical device" had to gain 510K approval from the FDA. At the time this was the largest medical system with this approval.

Defense Travel System

With the experience gained from my work with EDGAR and the ARC Blood Distribution System, large mission-critical systems be-came my specialty. In an earlier chapter, you read how I became involved with the Defense Travel System (DTS), which provides travel support for all civilian and military Department of Defense (DoD) personnel (air, hotel, car rental, and per diems.) The im-plementation of DTS was during the beginnings of the internet services at DoD and we had significant challenges with perfor-mance in many U.S. and foreign locations. I remember many tense meetings with high-ranking DoD officers discussing the "load" that the system put on the DoD infrastructure, especially the "last mile" and the military base infrastructure. We were convinced that web-based was the future and worked hard to improve performance, reduce the amount of data and work with DoD installations where performance was an issue.

"The Cloud"

A decade ago, if you asked any IT person whether they would prefer to host a large system in the cloud or in their own data center, undoubtedly, you would hear, "It is more secure in my own data center". However, 20 years later many government and commercial entities are providing cloud-based solutions. The advantages are clear as it is up to companies such as Amazon, Microsoft, Google, and IBM to manage and secure the entire infrastructure so that IT companies, such as Dovel, can concentrate on implementing the business solutions. Cloud companies spend enormous resources to continue evolving the cloud infrastructure and the various cloud tools that IT companies can use to enhance the solution offered to customers, but the transition is not pain-free. Some years ago, the push was to "move things to the cloud". However, applications were moved from one hosting solution to a different one without taking advantage of the cloud capabilities, and, as a result, the reputation of cloud-based solutions suffered. Over time, companies realized that the applications must be worked on, either redesigned, reimplemented, or at least modified, to take advantage of the cloud capabilities.

GrantSolutions.gov
Machine Learning and Artificial Intelligence

In 2016 I became the program manager of the GrantSolutions. gov[4] program, a system that handles volumes of grants on behalf of multiple government agencies. This is where I got much deeper into machine learning (ML) and artificial intelligence (AI) to address some specific needs. As with other technologies throughout my career, I wasn't a research and development type of person; rather, I was an executive who implemented solutions to address specific needs for which we selected the appropriate technologies and tools. There are multiple steps involved in the grant implementation processing for part of this process. First, there is a grant announcement, to which grantees respond. The government then assembles a team of experts who review and score the grants applications after grants are awarded. The process of reading and scoring the many applications is expensive and time-consuming, which is a significant business problem for our government customer. We researched whether ML could work as a solution to mitigate the resource-intensive process of reviewing and scoring the applications and found, after exploring many ML algorithms, that the technology was not (yet) sufficiently reliable. We learned, however, that ML could mitigate the problem by providing an opposite solution, that is, using ML could eliminate 50% of the applications from having to be read by a human, which is reliable and doable. So ML and AI do have a place in the federal space. But the human element shouldn't be underestimated, meaning that it can be threatening to the people who have been doing a given job for multiple years to hear that a machine can do the job. So significant care and attention must be given to the change management process in order to gain buy-in and make this successful.

Notes

1   https://en.wikipedia.org/wiki/XMODEM, accessed 12 January 2021
2   https://en.wikipedia.org/wiki/ZMODEM, accessed 12 January 2021
3   https://en.wikipedia.org/wiki/Standard_Generalized_Markup_Language, accessed 12 January 2021
4   www.Grantsolutions.gov, accessed 12 January 2021

7

TOLERATING RISK

Business ownership is not for the faint of heart.

Throughout the Dovel story, we faced significant environmental and economic threats, including loss of contracts, delays in contract awards, and resignations of senior executives, as well as federal decisions involving shutdowns, sequestration, and more. In the early phases the risks are greater as these challenges are most impactful, and, like for most entrepreneurs, our risk tolerance was tested often.

In this chapter, you will read about three areas of risk:

1. Financial
2. Resources and hiring (especially executive level)
3. Equity stake

We'll go through our decisions (failures to triumphs) during our organic growth and acquisition stages. As uncomfortable as our choices were, causing many sleepless nights, we learned that succeeding at entrepreneurship requires

- a high level of risk tolerance,
- the ability to be strategic in taking on risk,
- and managing risks.

Dov warns readers: Regardless of what business you're in, be assured that there will be challenges along the way. The key is that, to survive, you must learn to navigate, tolerate, and mitigate those risks to a manageable level.

DOI: 10.4324/9781003260653-9

Dov

The road from start-up through final transaction is not a beautiful linear progression. It certainly wasn't in our case, and traveling it required the ability to analyze and tolerate risk and mitigate its impact.

Some risky situations are under your control, but not all are, and as business founders, tolerating risk is a major factor. We are all different in how we deal with risk. In our case, Elma tended to ruminate and lay awake at night when stressful and high-risk matters arose, while for me, there isn't anything that gets between me and a good night sleep. Many nights I would wake up in the middle of the night and find Elma tossing and turning next to me. I often suspected that she was trying to get me to wake up as well, because as soon as I did, she would talk about whatever it was that kept her awake. It's not that I wasn't worried, but we process risk differently. I honestly think my way is better, or at least healthier, so usually I would answer, "Let's get some sleep so that we can better handle it in the morning". I knew that there wasn't a magic switch that she could turn on command, but what else could I say? As a wise person said, "95% of the things I worried about would not happen, so . . ." Over time, Elma established the following rules for herself, which was very helpful to her:

1. Imagine the worst possible outcome.
2. Decide what you are going to do about it.
3. Stop worrying, because you now know what to do should the worst come true (which usually doesn't).

Office Lease

Predicting is hard, especially about the future

– Yogi Berra

Initially, after outgrowing the attic, our corporate offices were in a shared office space in Bethesda called HQ. Regarding risk exposure, this worked well for us as the lease term was month to month. However, after adding offices over 18 to 24 months the total monthly cost no longer made sense, and we decided to make the big step to a multiyear lease. We learned quickly that any meaningful space would require a minimum 5-year lease, which equated to about $400,000 to $500,000 in total liability, and as we were a small business with limited assets, the landlord required that we, the owners, personally guaranteed the payment. This was a scary thought for us, planning five years out is challenging, and this liability is a risk for us. How to predict where Dovel would be in 5 years?

We followed Elma's rules on the worst-case scenario and decided that, should the worst happen, we had the resources to cover the required payment. We accepted the risk, signed the lease, and never looked back.

Government Contracting

A risk not under our control was the very real possibility of the government shutdowns we faced several times. Dovel's revenues come from people charging for work on government contracts, so any shutdown would have a significant impact on us, especially as a small business entirely in the government space, and with financial liabilities personally guaranteed.

What to do in a worst-case scenario and we faced a shutdown? Naively, we thought that the larger companies are better equipped to absorb such an impact that we could, so Elma reached out to a friend, who is a senior VP at a very large government contracting firm.

Elma: I still vividly remember this conversation: I was driving on the beltway on my way to the office in McLean, Virginia; this 30-minute commute was usually my time for thinking, planning, and talking. It's actually a wonder that I made this commute without accidents all these years, as my attention wasn't always fully focused on traffic. Anyway, I called my colleague/friend, a Sr executive at a large Government Contracting firm, and asked her if, in the event of a shutdown, they could place a few extra of our people on the contract. I will never forget her response: "No way, we are planning to furlough people". Call me naive, but I didn't know what this word meant, I had never heard it before. As soon as I arrived in the office, I googled the term *furlough* and was aghast. I walked over to Dov's office and said, "They're sending people home without pay! How will these employees manage?"

Furloughing people felt disloyal and disturbing to us, so we planned a different approach. We placed impacted people on overhead tasks and planned to reduce salaries (including our own). Fortunately, the shutdown was for a very limited time and involved only some of our work, but the experience taught us never to take revenues for granted, even on existing funded contracts.

Sometime later we were faced with a different scenario, one that, in hindsight, could have been avoided if the contract was managed better but ultimately still not something we had control over. One of our contracts with the Food and Drug Administration (FDA) was a task order (TO) contract; this meant that multiple tasks on the same contract were funded individually but were worked on by the same team. Unfortunately, when one or two TOs ended, there wasn't yet approval for the others, so part of the team had to be "benched", meaning, that we could not bill for them. Again, we didn't want to furlough or lay off, so we compensated these people from the profit of the active TOs. This gap in funding took all the profit from this contract for the year. I remember an unpleasant conversation with the contracting officer: I explained our dilemma, that terminating people from the team meant that, when TOs would be approved and funded, some of the people with knowledge of the program would not be available and that this would negatively impact the work but that we, as a small business, could not carry the burden of people on the bench for an extended period. She basically responded, "*Well, that's not our problem*", and she was right about that. We got through it and were able to keep the team intact, and we learned from it. We implemented monthly program management reviews to ensure senior-level oversight and advanced warning of at-risk programs.

Later, with Paul at the helm, we had to deal with the impact of another shutdown, as well as with sequestration. We decided to cut the salaries of all senior management, including ours, by 50% for a while; despite our initial concerns about how the team would react to this, it actually led to significant goodwill from the Dovel team, as they saw that we all shared the burden of avoiding furloughs or layoffs. It also became clear to the team that the common belief of better employment security at larger firms turned out to be a myth, as the larger firms implemented layoffs and furloughs, while at Dovel we absorbed the financial impact and managed the situation while keeping the team intact.

Calculating Risk of Investment

Every investment has risks and responding to a request for proposal (RFP) can be costly, so the decision must be made carefully and with as much information as possible. Around 2010–2011, Dovel had hit the wall of the growth slow-down phase, and something had to be done to get us through that phase and out of a slump. We learned of an opportunity at the FDA for which we were perfectly situated, with reasonable chances of success, if we allowed sufficient resources for the proposal effort. We seriously struggled with this decision because we knew that the general win rate of a response to an RFP was about 30% to 35%, and, although our fiscal situation was OK, allocating $50,000 to $75,000 was a major step. On the other hand, Dovel's direction would change if we were to win this contract: a 5-year, $58 million single-award prime contract, which would provide a significant increase in revenues, profit, and additional career opportunities for our team; a win would get us "over the hump".

Elma

After weighing the pros and cons we decided to go for it, and we went "all in". We retained a consultant, who, with his team as well as with Dovel employees, ran the proposal effort. This proposal effort took several weeks, and many weekend days and nights, but what I remember most is the night before the proposal delivery due date: our daughter, Karyn, who had been an intern at Dovel for a summer and had made her mark as a hard, smart worker, came home from college, and, straight from the airport, dove right in, supporting the team. One senior manager was about 8.5 months' pregnant at the time and sat with her legs up on a chair typing away. Paul, who had begun his CEO tenure just 4 days prior, was sent out in the evening looking for pre-punched printer paper, and I was told by my daughter (the only person daring to do so) to make coffee and stay out of the way: "Mom, we got this!"

The next morning Paul and Dov delivered the boxes with binders containing the precious proposal to the contracting officer at the FDA; the rest of us had been up the entire night, but we felt good about our work, and we were so proud of the team for the work they put in, regardless of the outcome.

Several weeks later we got the news that we had won! This was a turning point for Dovel, as this allowed Paul to hire the resources he wanted and to begin making changes to set Dovel on a new trajectory. Our investment had paid off! What would have happened if we had not won or if we had decided that the risk was too great? Well, we did submit the proposal and win, so. . .

Dov

Government contracting work includes advising the government customer on solutions and strategies, and many of our main contracts involved work on large mission-critical systems for the federal government, advising on, often followed by implementing, strategies that have major impact comes with significant risk.

Implementing a large mission-critical system is challenging because, due to its size and reach, it takes time to see positive results, and there are many stakeholders with conflicting agendas. As early as 2008, Dovel started capturing, analyzing, and reporting on all development projects. We had an outside expert review our data. We published an annual report titled *Dovel World-Class Quality*

Initiative, which highlights Dovel results compared to the rest of the industry. Our results were awesome! Multiple factors play a role, but I believe that a key factor is the ability to assess and mitigate risk. When proposing state-of-the-art solutions, we are cognizant of the fact that we are implementing large-scale solutions with significant impact; therefore, we make sure to consider according to "these technical components are available" versus "no one has ever put all these together before" We were always aware that our reputation depended on successful implementations of solutions and that, should something big go wrong, we would read about ourselves on the front page of the *Washington Post*. Whenever we read, or hear, about an IT government contractor involved in some big *clusterf*—, we say, there but for the grace of G. go we.

The following story illustrates program-level risks that are mostly beyond your control but nevertheless can impact you and your company.

At our program involving the Defense Travel System, we had an issue with the "last mile", that is, the connectivity between the Department of Defense (DoD) bases and the internet backbone.

The software had three modes: client/server, Telnet, and the web; remember that this is a few decades ago, with slower connectivity. At several DoD-wide meetings, we heard from high-level officers that our web mode put a load on the connectivity of national and global bases, and we were strongly advised to either work with Netscape to improve the compression or push the Telnet mode. We knew from experience that either choice was a bad one for one reason or another, so we took the risk and continued developing our web mode. Over time, connectivity improved, additional browsers became possible, and the system flourished. Clearly, it was very risky for us to go against recommended strategy, but we made a calculated decision and ultimately were successful.

Hiring the CEO

Finally, while these stories clearly illustrate various risk levels, the decision to bring in a CEO and hand over the company's steering wheel is at a whole different level. This transition is described in other chapters, so here the focus is only as it relates to risk.

We had many conversations about the pros and cons of bringing in a CEO, these questions were about the "why, when, how, and who" and about the inevitable "worst-case scenario".

Why: because clearly a change in direction was needed, requiring a different skill set
When: now is as good as ever. . .
How: consulting with legal, setting clear expectations, going "all in"
Who: Paul, of course
Worst case: The change in strategy proves fatal to the company, and Dovel doesn't not survive.

We had learned some lessons from prior senior-level hires that had not worked out well, and we were cautious because we know the damage a mistake can do to the culture, to us, and to the company. If the worst case had come true, it would have meant a significant loss for us, since we were still personally responsible for financial liabilities such as the lease and the line of credit; on the other hand, not making this move meant staying in a downturn (remember that we didn't know about the big FDA win yet), which could ultimately mean the demise of Dovel.

Clearly, we made the decision to go for it, and it was the right one (unfortunately that's only known in hindsight). We put measures in place to mitigate risk, and we decided to go "all in" to ensure that Paul, and we, would be successful.

Summary

Most people do not know about the near-death scenarios and the sleepless nights; why would they? But, as an aspiring entrepreneur, we want to make sure that you read this chapter carefully, because these are situations that occur, and many of these could easily have made Dovel go sideways.

8

THE BUSINESS DEVELOPMENT CHALLENGE AND CHASING RABBITS

"YES! We can do anything you want us to do!" These are tempting – and dangerous – words. It's easy to fall for this temptation at the start-up stage as you anxiously seek out the first customers.

Alternatively, your company may be at its growth stage when you or one of your overeager business development professionals chase every lead and make overreaching promises. Throughout Dovel's history and in the pre-Dovel days, we've experienced this temptation to *chase rabbits* (a term that Elma and I like to use).

Our advice: Don't chase *every* rabbit out there! In other words, avoid the "we can do everything" generalist approach. Focus on your core competencies.

DOI: 10.4324/9781003260653-10

Dov

I'm proud of Dovel's track record, and for being recognized in the industry for our core capabilities and strengths. At a very early stage we made the decision that we were going to be focused specialists in our field, because, as a small company, that's what would provide us the competitive advantage.

We recognized that IT start-up companies can go two ways: to become a general-purpose company that can do anything or to build, and be recognized for, deep expertise in specific areas with a deep background in adjacent core competencies. Based on our experience as a small company serving the government market, we believe that the second direction is best for gaining a competitive advantage. Over time, vertical expansion can be added to create growth.

So what this company should *not* do is get dragged into all the other types of technology work. Doing so will weaken the company's platform. They'd become known as the company that says it does everything. That may work for a very large company but not for a small or even midsized firm. In other words, sometimes you just have to say NO! Saying this can be hard to do, however, especially for us entrepreneurial types.

Here's another situation: Let's say you have a small firm specializing in government contracting. You approach a larger company to seek out subcontracting assignments from them, saying, "Our company can do everything that you can, and cheaper". But that reasoning is faulty. Why would a large company pay for you as a subcontractor when doing so ends up more expensive than they themselves doing that work in-house?

On the other hand, if your small company has a unique skill set in, for instance, machine learning (ML), artificial intelligence (AI), and cybersecurity, a larger company may wish to bring your firm in due to your highly specific core expertise.

The lesson here? As a small company you can't compete with the big guys. . . *unless* you go deep into a specialized skill set the big guys don't have!

Maintaining Focus With Your Business Development Efforts

As we have discussed earlier in this chapter, the more your company grows, the more you need to reassess your company's core strengths. Soul-searching and reevaluating should never stop. These assessments are particularly important once you reach the growth stage and add more members to your team. Doing this, you may feel a sense of déjà vu from your start-up days, particularly as your business development officer brings you opportunities that fall outside your company's core expertise, a mistake you used to make (but hopefully have stopped doing!).

This time around, your motive for saying, "Yes, we can do it", may be influenced by your desire to be encouraging and supportive of your business development group. However, your company runs the risk of (a) losing the bid because the competition has a better performance history or (b) winning the proposal but ultimately putting forth a weak performance due to lack of expertise required by this beyond-your-expertise project. So your company's reputation is very much on the line.

Growing to the Left and Right of Your Core Expertise

At some point in the life of a project, your customer may ask you if you can do a little something that is beyond your core expertise area. For example, you are developing software and the customer asks if you can help with operational aspects. That makes sense because your customer has come to trust you and wants to believe you can do many things . . . maybe everything!

However, you still must heed the danger of jumping into an unfamiliar project completely unrelated to your core expertise. Thus, it's time for more soul searching. So, again, ask yourself these questions:

- What do I want to be?
- What is my company's reason for being?

- What is *our mission* (there's that again. . .)?
- Who should we seek out to give us work?
- What kind of work should we seek?
- How can we attract the *right* talent to join our company?
- How are we going to keep them interested in *staying* with our company?

"Yes, We Can Do That"

As described earlier we experienced the fallout of saying "yes" without thinking it through early on when I agreed to find a developer with dBase III skills for our friend, the general manager at CompuMark USA, to build the trademark searching system. I was too eager to take on new projects and prove that I could do "anything", so I said, "Yeah, I can do that!" and it backfired awfully. Had I thought it through before agreeing, I would have recognized that I was already stretched too thin with a full-time job, and, more important, I did not know the computer programming language, no experience with dBase III at all. Because of this, I had to outsource the work, which resulted in the work not being completed by a time I had agreed to; I completed it myself after hours while learning this programming language. All's well that ends well, and the positive that came from this episode is, as described earlier, CompuMark gave us the confidence of a first project. We also learned valuable lessons:

- Trust but verify.
- Learn to say no.
- Stick with your core expertise.

Competencies and Business Stages

This experience with CompuMark impacted our thinking when we started Dovel later. We knew that our company's success in government contracting would depend on developing and selling core expertise rather than saying yes to every opportunity. We knew that our strengths were in developing and managing "Large Mission-Critical Full Life-Cycle Information Systems for the Federal Government"; this is where I gained my experience because of the Electronic Data Gathering and Retrieval (EDGAR) system, the American Red Cross (ARC) project, and, later, the Defense Travel System (DTS), and where I learned that these challenging programs require expertise and unique IT leadership skills.

What We've Learned

Start-Up Phase

To be competitive and to build the company's reputation, it is critical to establish your core expertise and focus on your value proposition, which will become your company's differentiator in a crowded field of start-up firms in whatever industry. As the company secures contracts and develops a reputation in the industry, enhance your competitive edge through vertical expansion of your business offerings. Your reputation becomes your business development tool because your team gets noticed for the high-quality work and customer-centric culture, and your team, being on the inside, can identify business problems for which you can offer solutions. By staying focused on developing your core expertise, you gain credibility as an advisor. This is how we build our reputation in the government contracting industry.

Dov

Pre-IDC/Dovel I managed a team of software development engineers for an $80 million, 70-person, 8-year project to build the Security and Exchange Commission's EDGAR system. That became my first experience with programs building mission-critical large-scale systems, and over time, I created a core team of experts, some of whom are still on our team today. As we became more experienced, we developed core strengths in all aspects of full

life-cycle development of large mission-critical systems: requirements, design, architecture, implementation, and operation for
software-intensive solutions. As technology rapidly evolved, each
new wave of technological innovations rapidly made previous ones
obsolete. We stayed on top of these new technologies, especially
as they pertained to our specialty of large systems. This is how
we became experts in service-oriented architecture (SOA), service-
oriented engineering (SOE), various cloud technologies, ML, AI,
and related technologies.

To market Dovel's core expertise within the government contracting industry, we took an alternative approach to traditional
business development. Our approach was to become trusted advisors to our customers. Being on the inside, working side by side
with our government customer, we recognized that they needed
solutions to actual business challenges and that they were open to
listening to us once we established trust and credibility by delivering quality work. They were also eager to learn what kind of solutions worked at other agencies.

One example illustrates this strategy: we recognized that our
DTS customer's business challenges could be served with an SOA
solution, but this approach is challenging to explain in a vacuum.
So, we created a "Lessons Learned" presentation, based on our
hands-on experience implementing a SOA-based system migrating
legacy systems to the cloud. We used this "Lessons Learned" presentation to explain this solution and how it would work for them.
We provided guidance and shared case examples of solutions we
worked on with other large-scale government agencies. Inevitably,
they would recognize that we knew of what we spoke, and they
would ask, "So, how can you help me?"

I'll add that participating as a speaker at industry conferences
was another effective way to promote our core expertise and build
credibility. After we completed a significant implementation of SOA
at the Department of Defense's Business Transformation Agency
(BTA), I was asked to speak about the project at an SOA sympo-
sium. Delegates from the Federal Aviation Administration (FAA)
were in the audience and spoke with me after the presentation.

I told them that we could come to their office and talk to them about the lessons we learned. We did, and several meetings later, we landed a contract at the FAA.

A downside of the trusted advisor approach is that the customer will insist that the advisor signs on as part of the team, we saw this increasingly as a contractual obligation. Obviously, this is not scalable, and over time, the limited availability of the key team is a major factor in the slowdown of the growth curve.

Growth Phase

As you ramp up your business development activities, and the company has an in-house business development (BD) team, stress the importance of remaining focused on the company's core strengths. Reassess what you want to be known for; think about your company's *mission and purpose.* Avoid the potentially damaging impact of going outside your comfort zone before you are ready. As described in the chapter on scaling/mission statements, the BD team wants to show success and bring in "wins", so they are tempted to go after every opportunity. Without guidance and oversight from management, you may find yourself with a contract for work outside the company's core expertise. At this phase, it is important to have a stable yet flexible BD process in place, with opportunities at the beginning and specific metrics and reviews along the way to full proposal delivery. Don't be afraid, as leader, to pull the plug if an opportunity isn't in the company's wheelhouse, or/and doesn't have a certain win probability. Once the team recognizes that the opportunities brought to the meeting will be vetted against specific parameters, using known metrics, they will be cautious in what they propose, and their presentations at the BD pipeline meetings with be focused and core expertise oriented. A process-oriented BD approach mitigates risks caused by emotions and personal pride. In our example, we didn't want to pour ice water on the enthusiasm of the BD team, so we went forward with an opportunity that wasn't within our core competencies. We won the work, a Continuity of operations (COOP) program contract, and we delivered, but it caused all kinds of problems and didn't gain us much in terms of long-term customer relations, growth potential, and competency building. Lesson Learned: by not wanting to say no, we experienced opportunity cost and internal strife.

At some point during this phase, many companies experience organic growth stagnation; most every aspect of the company works well, but the "growth engine" isn't working as it used to, and needs to.

At this point, a change in strategy is needed.

Maturity and Renewal Phase

What worked to get you to this phase probably will not work to get you through the next phase. This is when focusing on specific areas of the industry market becomes as important as the core competencies, and the BD process requires strong leadership to stay focused. In addition to increasing your presence through organic growth in existing markets, consider acquiring companies with the objective of expanding your footprint and/or strengthening your core expertise. Adding a strategy of *growth through acquisition* to your organic growth strategy is a major shift, which requires different strengths at the leadership level. For this chapter, let's focus on the acquisitions themselves and how they led to exponential growth and established Dovel as one of the largest midsized health information technology (IT) companies in the government space, at a time when this was a very desirable market to be in.

We found ourselves in health IT/life sciences market by design as well as by default: very early on, we were approached by a subcontractor who offered us an opportunity for a contract with the Food and Drug Administration, this led to several prime contracts at first and multiple others over the years. The most impactful was the Laboratory Information Management System (LIMS), a $58 million single-award contract. We decided to bid on this request for proposal (RFP), even though it was a significant risk for us because it required resources we couldn't afford, because the program was in our target market and the work was in our wheelhouse, so we went for it and won. Exactly at that time, we had decided on a shift in growth strategy, and over the next few years, we acquired two companies, both in health IT/life sciences (RNS/GrantSolutions in the Department of Health and Human Services and MSC at the National Institutes of Health). As a result of these strategic acquisitions, Dovel truly became known as a player in the government health IT domain. Paul Leslie, whom we brought in as CEO to lead the new strategy, clearly knew what he was doing, stayed focused, and guided the company to the next level.

Don't Chase Rabbits

While we changed strategies over the years, we remained committed to our core expertise. Our advice to entrepreneurs is the advice we've credited for Dovel's success: *do not chase rabbits.*

Be deliberate in deciding what you want your company to stand for and what the value is that you want your company to bring to the public. At first, the temptation is to accept any contract and any work that brings revenues, and sometimes you have no choice but to go for it because without revenues there is no company, but stay focused on your mission and don't stray too far from your path; at some point, you will look back and you see that you really build something meaningful, something that's true to the mission you set out in the beginning.

A Major BD Challenge: Hiring Business Developers

At some point during your company's growth phase, you bring in a BD team, and you begin by hiring a BD executive. This person will play a key role in your company, so you're looking for an experienced senior person who knows what they're doing and who has a track record of success. Our experience . . . easier said than done. We found that this was the most challenging role to fill, and we saw several BD executives come and go. We wanted so much to grow, and we knew that we needed help in the BD arena, that on many occasions and against our better judgment, we ignored red

Table 8.1 Salesperson Activities

Month	BD Executive activities
1–3	"I need to learn the company with all its core competencies so that I can approach the people on my Rolodex".
4–6	"I got it – now it is time to implement my marketing plan and approach the people on the Rolodex".
7–9	"Approaching the people on the Rolodex and going to bid on some RFP".
10–11	"Wow – it is harder than I thoughts, and most people on my Rolodex are no longer in the position where they can award business – we need to try a different approach".
12	"You guys expect too much, you are impatient, I can't work here . . . it's impossible".

flags and hired people who sounded too good to be true, and they were. At best, they didn't bring any new business to Dovel, and at worse, some of them left scars.

The story is typical, and we heard it many times from other business owners. The main challenge is that a small company does not have the resources to hire a good, reputable search firm to conduct a search for a business developer with a proven track record. Instead, we interviewed candidates whom we connected with through referrals or through efforts of our own recruiters. They all sounded good; they presented well and told us stories on how they won significant business for their previous employer, and about their amazing Rolodexes. We would check references, which were always glowing, check their previous places of employment, which always showed growth and we would ask multiple people to interview them and give us feedback. And still we cannot recall even one who created any meaningful business, but we do remember how much they cost us in compensation, as well as in opportunity cost and aggravation. We came to realize that their Rolodexes and the growth of their previous companies were not relevant to how successful they would be at Dovel. The challenge was that, if you looked at their past employment, indeed they showed growth. However, how much could this be credited to the candidate? And with respect to the Rolodex, this is the progress and timeline we experienced several times.

It was true that we were impatient because the compensation for these senior positions, and the expenses they incur for travel, meals, and so on were a significant drain on the company's resources, and despite us giving them the benefit of the doubt, again and again, we saw no results. We would start applying pressure after a few months. However, at some point, we would realize that another year had gone by with another "promising" business developer not delivering.

Turnover of senior people is not good for morale, reputation, and resources, and we had concerns about all of those and more, which led us to hold onto people too long sometimes. However, on several occasions, 12 to 18 months after a BD executive joined Dovel with great promise, we walked that person out the door with the regret of lost time.

Here are just a few anecdotal examples of our experiences:

- BD executive forecasts $2 million of new business revenues in Q1 of the next calendar, with ramping up; however, it's Q4 of the current calendar year without an actual plan of bidding, winning, and so on. Just a very confident forecast.
- BD executive has very poor judgment and shares very inappropriate "jokes" in front of potential customers and other staff.
- BD executive wins a contract with work that only he knows and proceeds to join up with a government employee to start his own business at our customer site, promoting his new gig on our time. We were later visited by investigators asking us questions about this; we knew it was unethical, but it turns out there was more to it that we unaware of. Luckily, we had let him go as soon as we recognized what was going on.
- BD executive is interested only in building an us-against-them fiefdom in the company, causing internal mistrust and instability. He isn't successful and leaves after a year.

Looking back, we were both too busy, Dov with overseeing and managing multiple projects and Elma with scaling and balancing the corporate governance. The BD didn't really fit in either of our swim lanes, neither of us really knew how and what to do to make it work, and we wanted desperately to believe that this third person could take it on and make it successful. Until we brought Paul in, we were unable to make it work.

With all the experiences and benefit of hindsight, we do not have advice on how to make this work, but we can share some thoughts:

1. If it sounds too good to be true – it is most likely is.
2. Be aware that semi-retired people who had successful careers may look at your company as a nice little place to be involved in while easing into retirement. It is wiser to hire people who are early in their career and have something to prove.
3. Ask the candidate if they would consider a low salary and a high upside. Someone who agrees to this has confidence in their ability to get new business and earn upside.
4. A candidate from a large company will expect resources and infrastructure that you and your small company do not have and cannot afford. They will blame the lack of this infrastructure for their failure to be successful.

The founders are usually the best BD people; however, we recognize that this is not scalable. Unfortunately, we do not have the answer for you. We ultimately decided to hire a CEO and let him deal with it, because we were exhausted.

9

LETTING GO

We vividly remember a conversation many years ago when a member of our advisory board asked us with respect to letting go of control: "How will you react when your CEO makes decisions that you disagree with?" That got us thinking about the complexity of "letting go". But, as it turned out, once we made the decision to bring in a CEO to implement a different growth strategy, we were determined to make it work and did everything possible to ensure success. This seems simple, but although it was successful, it wasn't always easy, and not everyone can make this adjustment. As you read this chapter, you should ask yourself, "How would I react to 'letting go' of control?"

DOI: 10.4324/9781003260653-11

Letting go of people, places, things, and the familiar, is a necessary, but often difficult, process in life. To understand the process of letting go, we've learned to come to terms with the experience. Like everyone, we've had to feel the emotional pain of sadness and mourning. We've had to deal with our fears and perceived threats. We realized that we might suffer failure and the aftermath of letting go too soon, too much, or not enough. Letting go is hard work: you need to muster all the trust, courage, and optimism you can find within. But the good news is that the hard work is worth the effort in the end.

Letting Go to Move Forward

Elma: Through my early life experiences, I had associated the process of letting go with moving forward to something else, taking a step ahead to something new instead of running away from something. As we shared earlier in this book, Dov moved to Washington, D.C., in December 1981 for his graduate studies. Meanwhile, I had accepted a nursing job that would start in January 1982 at a university hospital in Amsterdam. At that point, I never thought that I would ever leave The Netherlands and move permanently to another country. However, my life took unexpected turns as I adjusted to letting go.

Looking back on my life over that period, I was continuously letting go of the familiar to go toward something new. In 1982, I left behind my family, my home, and my native country to settle in the U.S. with Dov. My family and friends missed me, and I missed them, as well as my home and familiar surroundings, very much. Plus, I was frightened by the immigration experience. Nonetheless, later that year, I let go of my single life and married Dov. A few years later, I left my Catholic faith and converted to Judaism. Fast-forward to 2000, I left a career in nursing, and that year became a cofounder of a start-up IT business with Dov. Later again, I let go of my role as CEO and my day-to-day involvement with the company.

What did I learn from my transition from a Dutch Catholic nurse to an American Jewish business executive? I recognized the need to

a.   deal with risk
b.   trust that, no matter what was ahead, I would be okay; and
c.   embrace new opportunities and feel excited about moving forward in my life.

Each time, I decided to be "all in" despite my discomfort and apprehension during my life transitions. Letting go of the past was essential for my personal growth and development.

Parenting and Learning How Much to Let Go

Dov: When I was a child, I grew up in a "moshav", a small community with only 33 families and plenty of open spaces. Together with the other children, we could freely roam around without parental supervision. We played and made a little mischief (nothing serious). That was childhood life in Israel during the early 1960s, in a small community near the beach. When I became a parent, however, my children lived in the U.S. in a major metropolitan area and a different time.

As Elma and I became parents, we often discussed how much freedom to give our children, Karyn and Mark. How much should we allow our children to experiment, and perhaps fail, so they would learn and grow into independent adults? We tried to decide how much we should let go and at what times.

When our daughter, Karyn, was in her senior year in high school, she began talking about her plans after graduation. Karyn declared that she had done her research, and found that she could survive on a waitress's salary in Montana and skip college altogether.

My father had practically forced me to attend college when I was my daughter's age. Looking back on my early life, I am thankful for my father's decision to maintain some control over my plans. Elma and I consider education as one of the most critical and impactful decisions in a person's life. When Karyn showed no interest in college, I decided that it was time to step into action. While Elma was away for a few days, I presented my daughter with a challenge. I told her that I would pay her $100 for each college application that she would complete and submit. This plan was my way of giving her room to make her own decisions but still guide the way. Rather quickly, Karyn completed five college applications. All five colleges offered her a place, and one even offered her a partial scholarship. She never asked for the money, attended and completed college and is now a successful Sr SW Engineer.

Starting a Company Means Becoming a Parent All Over Again

As parents of children, and cofounders of a company, we have recognized striking parallels during the life stages of both. From the day we cofounded Dovel, we nurtured and guided our company through the four life-cycle stages of all businesses: (1) start-up, (2) growth, (3) maturity, and (4) rebirth/renewal (we avoided decline).

Like with children who grow up, when Dovel matured from a start-up to a successful mid-tier company, we knew that gradually giving up control of day-to-day operations was necessary for the ultimate well-being of the company. Watching its growth and development, like we've watched our children become strong independent adults, has been one of the best parts about being Dovel's "parents". However, as we said earlier, the "letting go" process came with ups and downs as we worked our way toward Dovel's full maturity and ultimate acquisition.

If you are, or have been, the owner of a company with full decision-making control, you likely recognize what we experienced. To successfully move the company forward, each stage of a company's life cycle requires a different leadership style. A leader who brings certain strengths at the start-up stage, when organization, flexibility, vision, and culture are important, may not be the best person to get your company through the next phase, which may require negotiating skills, a certain level of detachment from day-to-day operations, and a different network of connections. We learned that our strengths were ideal for the start-up and rapid growth stages, but the maturity stage required other skill sets. For the health of the company, we had to begin letting go of controlling Dovel, incrementally, and that was a humbling, painful experience. However, we accepted this reality and focused on the best interests of our company. We brought in new leaders with the strategies and expertise that moved Dovel to the next stages. If our pride and ego would have prevented us from accepting the fact that different leadership was required, Dovel's story could have likely ended differently.

The Exchange: Letting Go of One Career to Start Another

Elma: In January 2000, we began our business cofounder partnership. Integrated Data Corporation (IDC) had been in existence since the fall of 1986 and was initially run by Dov and a business partner before Dov became the sole owner. In January 2000, Dov convinced me to become the cofounder. I let myself take the plunge but not without concerns.

I recall my conversation with Dov. I explained that I was not going to do "back office" support. I had to be an equal partner. We agreed on our equity: 51% for me, 49% for Dov. Meanwhile, I was deeply concerned about what running a business together would do to our marriage and family. Added to that worry, I was apprehensive about losing my identity, standing in Dov's shadow was not my ideal objective. However, I allowed my trust to guide me. I had to think optimistically and share enthusiasm about the potential growth and success of this new business that we now owned together.

Somehow it all came together and swiftly. Within the same period of a few months, I let go of my health care career, sold our house, renovated our new home, and began setting up a corporate structure for our new company. That was it. I moved forward to a new career, a new place, and a new role and never looked back.

Bringing on Our First Employees and Specialists

Elma: I had no experience working in an office, let alone working with government contracts. However, I moved ahead, learning as I went along, and put IDC/Dovel's structure in place. The time arrived, however, when I had to come to terms with the necessity for new employees to help me with administrative duties. Initially, I couldn't (or did not want to) imagine that anyone had my skills to process an invoice or review a contract or reconcile a bank statement. I had to get over the idea that only I could do the work and do it correctly. I had difficulty hiring the first employees. I had to find a "trust but verify" balance: overseeing and being supportive without micromanaging and checking their work every minute.

I made a couple of rules that helped me adapt to having a team:

1. "Do it my way or do it better". If you don't do the job better, you may as well do it my way.
2. "We'll never *knowingly* do something that isn't right". As the company grew, I had to develop the culture and processes. Integrity and ethics were top on my list. Government contracting comes with so many Federal Acquisition Regulation (FAR) rules that made it impossible for us to know everything. It's okay to use the best judgment and still make mistakes, but never *knowingly* do something wrong.
3. There are no mistakes, only learning experiences. Allow the team to make mistakes and talk about it so everyone learns.
4. "If there are overlaps, then there must be gaps" in the workflow. Efficiency was also high on my list of objectives. If multiple people were doing the same work (an employee issue: delegating), then for sure there must be work that is not getting done.

I made the process of handing off my duties a little easier by becoming a sort of "orchestra conductor". As I brought on more employees and accounting specialists, we all went by our standard process and procedures and adjusted them as we scaled the company.

Our transition to a more sophisticated accounting system took me out of my small business QuickBooks comfort zone. My ability to trust and rely on the staff was put to the test. Our company was growing, and our professional accounting staff was best suited to manage our needs. In other words, I realized that others were more qualified than me to manage and lead certain aspects of the business.

Bringing Executives to Our Team: What We Learned

The concept seemed simple enough: if you want to move your business from the start-up to growth stages, you need to expand your leadership team. However, Dov and I learned the complexities of doing this – through a few hits and misses! – when we hired executives to join us at the time that Dovel was still in the small-company stage. As we were developing Dovel's infrastructure, we wanted to be careful in our executive hires. We had to consider the cohesiveness of our staff and our company's future. These points guided us along the way:

- Decide as cofounders the key strengths, that is, operational strengths and negotiation strengths, that we needed to add to our existing team.
- Discuss your expectations internally: Why are we bringing in someone at this level? What value are we expecting this person to add?
- Look for the right combination of leadership skills, industry knowledge, and personality that would work well in the company's culture.
- Ensure that you and the candidate have an understanding and agreement on the purpose and goals of the role.
- Make sure you provide clarity about the company's values and your strategic goals during the interview process.
- Do not ignore the "red flags" in your eagerness to fill the role!
- Stay united as the founders. Avoid triangular dynamics.

When Letting Go Got Tougher: The New CEO

Dov: By 2010, Elma and I were getting tired. We were putting in long hours at work, yet we had no idea what Dovel's future would look like. Also, we recognized that we would have to adjust our growth strategy to avoid stagnation and possible decline. Around that time, one of my business acquaintances, who served as the CEO of another company, approached us and expressed an interest in acquiring Dovel. The idea was appealing, but I realized that I would be working even harder as the CTO [chief technology officer] of the acquiring company. Elma and I agreed to pass. Meanwhile, another possibility would soon develop with someone I knew from the EDGAR days: Paul Leslie.

Elma: In the fall of 2010, our advisory board was in place and holding semiannual meetings. Dovel was experiencing stagnating growth. At that point, we were talking about adding an acquisition strategy in addition to organic growth. I asked Paul Leslie, an advisory board member, to be my senior advisor for several months. He agreed. We all enjoyed having Paul with us during those months. Paul advised Dovel's acquisitions strategy, and we all decided that this strategy shift would require a management change, including a CEO with the leadership skills to implement an acquisition strategy successfully. I told Paul, "We assume that Dovel would be too small for you, right?" Paul surprised us by saying that he would consider it if his other pending offer did not go through.

Dov: At that time, Paul was in talks with a private equity firm about becoming the CEO of a company it was interested in acquiring. Initially, we were skeptical that Paul would even consider becoming a CEO of a small company like ours. But Paul said all the right things: "I don't care about a high salary, but I do want ownership in the company". He said he wanted to do "one more deal", referring to a previous deal in which he successfully implemented the acquisition strategy.

Elma: Two months later, Dov and I vividly remember being in Boston for our daughter Karyn's graduation. We received a text message from Paul: "The deal fell through". We texted back, "Awesome, can you start Monday?" Indeed, Paul started that Monday.

Paul became our CEO and Elma became the Chair of the Board that following Monday. That same week, we completed and submitted a proposal to the Food and Drug Administration, and a few weeks later, we learned that Dovel won a $58 million single-award contract. We felt like proud parents whose child had just graduated from college with top honors (which, coincidentally, also just happened). This new contract was a massive win for our team, especially for Paul. He would now have the bandwidth and resources to hire the team of professionals he wanted at salaries that we were never able to pay in the past. Dovel was on its way, and in good hands with Paul as CEO.

Elma's Challenges

Elma: I should have been ecstatic about having a new CEO, and I was. However, I continued to go to my office every day from May until August, trying to figure out how to best work through this transition. Those months were difficult for me, as I realized that I was no longer in charge, and I felt no longer relevant! I kept reminding myself that this was what I wanted and what was best for Dovel to move to the next level. At first, I handed over operational information to our new human resources (HR) director, new director of accounting, and other senior managers.

Toward the end of August, I had a conversation with the new HR director. I could sense that she was confused about who was in charge. At that moment, I understood that I should no longer be there. (I think I cried when that realization hit me.) It was Wednesday afternoon, the middle of the workweek. I went home around 3 o'clock and didn't go into the office for the rest of the week. I was not angry or hurt, but it was suddenly clear to me that something had to change, I had to change On the following Monday, I returned to the office. I told Paul that he should move into my office, take my desk, and sit in my chair. _Optics mattered_. The team had to "see" who the captain on the ship was. I took a side table in Dov's office, realizing that I had to figure out what to do next. How could I remain relevant at Dovel? What do I do now?

Meanwhile, Dov and I experienced conflict. We each wanted what the other had. I saw that Dov was still very much involved and relevant. Dov, on the other hand, envied my freedom. This transition ultimately, and perhaps inevitably, brought conflict among Paul, Dov, and myself (where I usually was the mediator).

Dov's Challenges

Dov: So, how hard was it for me to adjust?

Paul is not a technical person, so he wanted me to stay in charge of the technical team. However, I had to accept a significant change in my role and freedom. It was no longer Dov and Elma doing what we wanted. There was a third voice now.

When Paul joined Dovel, he brought new senior leadership, including a vice president of business development. I'll admit it, we butted heads several times. We were running a project at the U.S. Census Bureau and had some issues due to shifting requirements on the customer side. What was new to me was that I had to explain things and try to convince others of what strategy to follow rather than just tell others how things should be done. In hindsight, I realized that the conflict involved more than a disagreement about the proposal, it wasn't easy for me to have to consider others' opinions. Bottom line: We lost the procurement.

"Wow", I said to myself. "Life is going to get a lot more complicated around Dovel. Where do I fit in now? Am I working for someone else now? What is my role?" It seemed to me that Paul was saying, "We want you to be our top lead guy, but you are not making the decisions alone". Elma's challenges were different. She felt left out of her day-to-day duties altogether.

At that point, I remembered a discussion that we once had with one of our board members, a highly experienced executive in a publicly traded company. When we talked to him about the possibility of hiring a CEO, he said: "Think about this scenario. What will you do if the CEO you hired wants to spend half a million dollars on something and you disagree?" That question didn't seem so difficult in the abstract. But once we were in the middle of it, it was not easy.

At home, Elma always had a way of bringing me down to earth. There were many evenings when I came home talking about work and saying something like, "This is so complicated", implying that I was the *only* person who could fix the issue. Elma would usually respond by saying something along the lines of "Go and take the trash out. Remember, you are just like everybody else". That was Elma's way of reminding me that I wasn't indispensable.

Embracing Our New Life

Elma: Dov and I were not letting go of the past way of doing things. As CEO, my strength was as an operational manager. Paul's strengths, on the other hand, were strategic. Logic would have told us that keeping the status quo would have been detrimental for Dovel and our employees. We both understood that we did not bring Paul on as CEO to approach the role as I had.

I wanted this transition to work, so I engaged a business counselor for Dov and me to untangle some of the conflicts. We were finding this helpful. However, by November, I suggested to Dov that we go away for several months and give the team space to figure things out without us. Dov and I rented an apartment in Tel Aviv for 8 incredible weeks! We had productive weekly Skype sessions with Paul.

When we returned to the States, and the office, we still had occasional tensions. However, we noticed that everything seemed different, better, and we knew our roles. Dov and I were on our way toward letting go. In a way, we were becoming empty nesters, all over again. Instead of the children leaving home, we were leaving our company so that it could have a better future.

We started enjoying our new life and freedom. Dov and I got busy renovating our new apartment, selling our house, downsizing, and moving. I became involved in community volunteer activities and started my own leadership coaching business.

As we moved along, I could look at the situation objectively and understand my rationale for bringing in a CEO to replace me. But it didn't make the transition less painful. People often tell me that they fully understood what I was going through: I was giving up my baby.

But here's what I tell them: I wasn't giving up my baby; I gave up my 10-year-old child! After spending a decade putting all my energy and effort into raising, educating, and nurturing my child, someone came in and said, "Let's put some decent clothes on this child and give it a better education!"

I would advise anyone in a similar position: remember why you decided to let go. Stay focused on the ultimate objective.

Our Lesson on Trusting

'If you start to take Vienna, take Vienna!' (Napoleon Bonaparte)

Once you decide to hire a CEO, then hire a CEO. Avoid the temptation to "play it safe" by hiring your "CEO choice" and placing them in a lower role to see if they work out; it won't work out in most cases, because a highly qualified and experienced person is not likely to tolerate being "under observation" for very long and leave. While we knew that our approach was risky, we felt that it was the right way to go about it: we decided to hire Paul as CEO, so we hired Paul as CEO and gave him significant control over the company.

"I hope he knows what he's doing" (Dov and Elma).

We knew that hiring a CEO was the right thing to do and that Paul was the right person. But we were struggling to let go of the way we had done things in the past. We had to let trust and optimism guide us. One thing we were certain of, the most important quality: with Paul, we never had to doubt that he was making decisions for the right reasons and for the best of the company and the team. Until the end, Dovel was known for its culture of integrity, and Paul was the right fit for this environment.

We simply had to learn to trust and tolerate risk. Paul began investing by hiring overhead staff and paying salaries that we would have never dreamed that we could have afforded to pay in the early years. This was difficult for us. We went with it, even though we challenged him from time to time, but we never said, "No". The three of us had many open conversations. We had always been cautious fiscally in how we managed Dovel, weighing each hiring decision carefully. "Why do we need this person? Why do we need five people in business development? What is the rate on return?" We decided that we were going to trust what Paul was doing and support his decisions. It took a while for us to feel comfortable with the ever-expanding overhead. We kept saying to each other, "What is happening? The expenses are growing, but we don't seem to be expanding business". However, we eventually decided that we were going to trust and let go, as scary as it sometimes was for us.

People have asked us, "With your very conservative approach towards money and spending, how did you deal with the radically different strategy of taking on loans and liabilities to finance the acquisitions?" The truth is, we made a very deliberate decision to implement a very different strategy for the good of the company, even though this was way out of our comfort zone and risky. We had made the decision, gave up most of our compensation to support the investments in the growth of the company, and learned to live with the risk of potentially losing it all. At the time we didn't know where this would lead, but, as it has turned out, everything has worked out beautifully.

10

PREPARING FOR EXIT

There are many aspects to a transaction, and we could write an entire book on that subject alone. Here we focus on the highlights of the two main categories: corporate and personal. We know, because of our experience, that the personal side can easily be forgotten until much too late, but it is just as important, and like the corporate side, where there are many expert entities involved, there are experts to guide you, but finding your personal "exit team" will take time. Our advice: establish a wealth management team way in advance, so you will have qualified support to guide you.

DOI: 10.4324/9781003260653-12

PREPARING YOUR COMPANY FOR EXIT

Elma

In my role as a business coach/mentor, I work with business owners who are in the start-up and growth stages of their companies. When I mention exit strategies or endgames, the typical response is: "I don't even want to think about that yet, I am having fun for now". The reality is that the time to plan your endgame is sooner than you think, as in several years before an actual transaction. To prepare your company for the mergers and acquisitions (M&A) market, you need to have a good idea what that market will be looking for and how to make your company an attractive target.

You probably will not know yet whether you will gravitate toward a strategic buyer or a private equity (PE) buyer, and this may not matter to you at any time, but there are some ways in which they differ, and how you prepare may matter. Think about how important it is for you and your team to keep the company name, and to keep the management team intact, rather than let go of staff and absorb the company to create efficiencies.

The descriptions below are solely based on *our experience* with Dovel as the acquirer, as well as the target.

Strategic Acquisition

A strategic acquisition is a transaction in which the buyer is interested in acquiring your company for strategic reasons; you may have a unique product or service that they need to complement or expand their offerings, and which will be more efficient for the buyer to acquire than to build in-house. To package your company for this, think about developing assets like a "secret sauce", like proprietary methodologies that make your company attractive to a buyer because it will save them money and/or resources or it solves a problem. Be strategic in developing this asset, just because you think it's great, doesn't necessarily mean that it's valuable to a buyer. Make sure that you protect your proprietary asset and that you have quantifiable metrics to show its impact and value.

If it's your core services that make you desirable, make sure that you are known for these services and that you have stayed focused on becoming the best in that field. For example, if your company sells cyber security consultancy services, make sure that your core is all about that. In the information technology (IT) industry, the "knowledge" industry, the ability to build and retain key players with highly desirable skills can be attractive to a buyer, so incentivize and engage your team.

The other reason a strategic buyer can be interested in your company is your active pathway into an attractive market; in the government contracting industry, this means full and open (F&O) contracts in agencies of interest to the buyer. The value of F&O contracts is significant, because the buyer will most likely not be a small business or have any other set-aside status. Most start-ups have contracts with set-aside status, as defined by the Federal Acquisition Regulation: small, veteran-owned, women-owned, and so on. This set-aside status is dependent on the status of 51% or more of the equity holders, for example, a "women-owned small business" set-aside company can hold contracts specifically for that category if 51% or more of the equity is held by women; however, once a large buyer acquires the company, this category no longer holds. What this means is that set-aside contracts do not have value in the context of M&A, no matter how profitable or strategic they are. With respect to the markets or agencies of interest, this depends entirely on the buyer; some are interested in commercial markets, some more in government markets, some focus on defense, and others on civilians.

So, to prepare your company for a strategic buyer,

- develop proprietary assets and prepare impact reports that show value;
- stay focused on your core competencies and develop unique skills;
- grow, and become known, in specific markets; better to be large in few than small in many; and
- in government contracting, convert your set-aside programs to F&Os.

PE Acquisition

A PE transaction is different from a strategic buyer, in that the buyer is interested in a "change of control", without necessarily absorbing or running the company. The change of control refers to the PE firm acquiring enough equity to become the majority stakeholder, generally more than a 70% to 75% stake in the company. The objective is to acquire, recapitalize, grow, and resell. The benefit to you, the owner, is that you will be paid for your equity, you're "cashing out", or "taking money off the table", while your company usually remains intact. This is an easier message to your team, and it significantly lessens your risk. The downside, because there always is one, is that you are no longer the majority decision-maker, which can be unsettling, because the objectives of the decision-makers are different from yours. It's exciting to have the capital to significantly grow your company, until you realize that it's not really "your company" anymore. PE firms refer to this type of target company as a "Platform Company", the first acquisition made by a PE firm in a specific industry or market, with the objective of creating a foundation to absorb additional acquisitions. They grow this family of companies organically, as well as through additional acquisitions, until they sell to either another PE firm, or to a strategic buyer.

The PE firm is not interested in running day to day operations, so they look for a company with a strong, experienced management team with a proven track record of growth, a strong presence in a desirable market, and a more mature organization with defined systems and standard operating procedures that match the investment criteria of the private equity firm.

So, to prepare your company for a PE buyer,

- develop a mature executive and management team, with structured governance and oversight;
- stay focused on your core market and your competencies; and
- establish and socialize flexible, yet resilient business processes that are strong enough to provide structure, yet adaptable enough to absorb growth without imploding.

Why Is It Important to Know What Kind of Transaction You Are Looking At

Valuation

Company founders usually don't think they need an external valuation of their company. Let's face it, it's expensive, company resources are scarce, and besides, they already "know" how much their company is worth, and they won't sell for a penny less. It's a well-known fact that founders usually overestimate the value of their company, much like new parents usually overestimate the cuteness (and brilliance) of their kids. The founder will come up with a number based on XX (a number they've heard in the marketplace) times EBITDA (earnings before interest, taxes, depreciation, and amortization), and that's "the Number". Obviously, at the time of transaction, the value is what the buyer agrees to pay.

When and Why Is a Valuation Important?

- An external valuation serves as a healthy dose of realism.
- It provides the owner(s) with insight into what adds/negates the value of the company, and this information could drive exit strategy.
- If you plan to add additional equity stakeholders, it is important to have an external report that confirms the value of each share/unit. The new equity holder will buy the equity based on the value as determined with the valuation, if this valuation was done within a certain amount of time, and there haven't been any meaningful changes; this is the "basis", the difference between the basis (price when the equity holder buys the equity) and the final share/unit value at transaction time is capital gain.

We hired a company to come in and do an external evaluation for personal estate planning purposes, more on that later. When Paul joined us as the third equity stakeholder, after Dov and me, we used that valuation because not too much time had gone by and not too much had changed. That valuation provided the basis for Paul's equity; for Dov and me, the basis was zero.

Take Care of Your Team: The Equity Bonus Plan

In planning for an exit, don't forget your team!!

We implemented the Equity Bonus Plan to reward the team for their tremendous efforts and to show them the recognition that we did not do this alone and that, without the hard work of many leaders in the company, Dovel's journey would not have been as successful. This belongs in this chapter because taking care of your team must be part of your exit planning. In October 2021, we celebrated the final closing of the sale of Dovel to Guidehouse, and we have confirmation that, with this plan, we accomplished the objective of rewarding key people on our team in a meaningful way.

At the time of strategy change, when we brought Paul in as CEO, we recognized that we needed a plan to attract, retain, incentivize, and reward our senior management, but we wanted to avoid equity dilution. In addition, giving someone equity is a taxable event for the recipient, which we wanted to avoid (we know that there are other ways to grant stock, but we wanted to keep things simple). So we, together with our Cooley Team, put together a plan we called the Equity Bonus Plan. In short, we determined that the plan value consisted of 10% of the net proceeds of a "change of control" transaction; the pool held initially 100,000 points (later, as we grew, this became 200,000) we called EBUs (Equity Bonus Units). The points were awarded on a merit basis, they were not portable (if someone left the company, the points would return to the plan), and their value depended entirely on the value of the company at the time of transaction.

Before the 2019 transaction, in which the equity holders sold 90% of their equity to a major PE firm, I'm not sure people recognized the value of the EBUs. I think some may not even have remembered that they had them, or how many, so in terms of incentivizing and retaining, this may not have the most effective solution, but in terms of rewarding, it worked: at the 2019 transaction, the pool was worth over $15 million, which was distributed to more than 26 participants. Almost all participants reinvested their after-tax gain back in Dovel, with partial matching by the buyer. The end result is that plan participants received significant rewards at the final transaction in October 2021. If there is anything that makes us most proud, and almost emotional, it's this . . . the fact that so many of our team received well deserved financial rewards at impactful, life-changing levels. Nothing made us happier than that!

Dov

Are You Ready for a Transaction?

For many founders, the exit is the ultimate objective; for others, it's something that they gradually come to recognize as an option to take money off the table and enjoy a little more freedom.

Either way, you will need to get comfortable with the concept from all angles, because, even though the company will have others at the senior level, you, as the majority owner, have the deciding vote. Sounds simple, right? Well, from our experience, there were many ups and downs along this road, and it was good that Elma and I agreed beforehand about the right path and the right time for us.

Establishing a Target Sale Price

Clearly, for the founder(s), the price at which you are willing to hand over control of your company is an emotional concept, so the value must be determined in an objective way. Earlier in this chapter, Elma talked about the valuation process, which is one way to establish an objective value; another way is to talk to an M&A broker, and, if you are comfortable, you can "test the market" by talking to potential buyers. If the value you are set on does not align with the objective valuation, you will need to either adjust your expectations or abandon the process altogether.

The Transaction Process

A "change of control" transaction, one in which you as the founder will go from majority equity holder to minority equity holder, is a long and exhausting process, and if you're not careful, it can impact the morale and culture of your team and the health of your company. Members of your senior leadership will be asked to gather information and participate in multiple management meetings with potential buyers, in addition to their regular responsivities. Remember, the company needs to continue its healthy growth trajectory to remain a target for buyers, and if the transaction falls through, you don't want to look back and find that you just lost 6 to 9 months' worth of opportunity. Also, most transactions will have some form of target-based "earn-out", so you must make sure that the company is on track to meet these targets.

Until the very end, meaning, until the hour when the signatures are set, this process is highly confidential. This can be stressful by itself because this might be the most impactful event in your professional, and to some extent your personal, lifetime, and you will not be able to talk about it with most people in your circle.

In May 2019, Elma and I sold 90% of our equity stake in Dovel Technologies. At the time Paul was our CEO for several years already, and Dovel was prepared for an exit with PE: mature management, desirable market, sound governance, and strong foundation to serve as a "platform" company. The transaction was labeled a recap, rather than an acquisition, because the PE firm, Macquarie Capital, did not plan to absorb the company, run operations, and change the name.

The transaction process had been exhausting, the senior team met with more than 10 companies, each meeting lasting multiple hours, during which the team presented Dovel, and the potential buyer talked about who they are and why they were interested in Dovel, as well as what their post-transaction plans would be. Some are honest, while others tell you what you want to hear. Regardless, post-transaction the new controlling equity stakeholder can, and will, do what it set out to do; in the case of a PE company, this means maximizing its return on investment.

The Transaction Day

Dov

The day of the transaction I went to my office in Rockville, where I was the Sr Advisor to the GrantSolution program . . . the work had to continue, and there was no practical reason for me to be in the corporate office in McLean.

Elma: The transaction closing was scheduled for a Tuesday; however, one document still needed to be signed, so Tuesday the transaction did not happen.

On Wednesday morning, I went to the office in McLean to be together with everyone, a bottle of champagne ready to go; the final event was scheduled to be around 10 a.m. Around 9:15, the senior team was in the office, and multiple lawyers were on the conference call; we're ready to go. Everyone confirmed that they had what they needed to close the deal . . . until we heard that the office in Delaware, where the final "stamp of approval" needed to come from, was going to close for training at 9:30, so no closing that day. Thursday, at 8:30 a.m., I am at home with only my golden retriever, Rosie (Maggie had passed away years before), keeping me company; now there is nobody in the corporate office; we're all on the conference call. The deal closed, and I burst into tears, feeling as if a huge weight just came off me. Rosie came over and put her head on my lap.

The Post-Transaction Company

Dov

As the founder, I had strong views, and mixed feelings, about my post-transaction role. On the one hand, it felt good to be considered indispensable, and critical to the future success of the company. However, if I over-emphasized the importance of my role, the buyer would want to protect their investment and put agreements in place to ensure that I stay. My view of a post-transaction life did not necessarily revolve around the company, and I wanted to ensure that I had options. So I had to reduce my visibility and lessen the importance of my role in the months leading up to the transaction. I swallowed my pride so that the success of the transaction did not include a binding agreement with me.

Non-competes and All That Jazz

The buyer just spent a significant sum to acquire control of Dovel, and they must protect their investment. For this, we had multiple attorneys debating how to mitigate the risk of every possible scenario, and regardless of your intentions, they will want to make sure that it is all in one of the agreements. Since I was continuing in my role as a senior advisor to a major Dovel project, there was significant back-and-forth on the duration of my employment and my status, restrictions, and postemployment activities. We had no intention, or desire, to start another company and compete with Dovel, but for obvious reasons, all the scenarios that posed actual and potential risks to the new ownership had to be legally papered over with "non-competes". We understood why this was necessary, but it felt invasive and overly restrictive and eroded some of the good feeling around this event.

Elma: Even though my role at the company was at an entirely different level than Dov's, there were non-competes for me to sign because of my work as a business coach and mentor; again, we understood their concerns, but we also were somewhat irritated by the need to paper every possible scenario; after all, they were taking over our company . . . what did they think we would do to harm its success? It's hard to say, "It's nothing personal, it's just business", when you're selling a life's work.

What bothered me more was the fact that there were no women at all in this transaction, and there would be no women on the new Dovel Board at all! This was of great concern to me for many reasons, too many to elaborate on in this book. So I insisted on a board seat, something that took a little convincing. To boost my confidence, and to add to my credentials, I completed a weeklong program for Women on Boards at the Harvard Business School. The quarterly board meetings were eye-openers because it was very clear that the objectives of the new owners were so unlike ours; once again, we had to accept change for the better.

Legal Representation

The number of attorneys involved is in direct relation to the size and complexity of the transaction. We advise founders who find themselves in a transaction to get their own legal representation, one who has only your best interest at heart. You may think that the attorneys representing your company should be sufficient, but they represent the company, not you. We are so grateful that we retained our own lawyer, who looked out for our best interest, especially with all the non-competes and the like.

A Second Bite of the Apple

Generally, the PE group wants the equity stakeholders to stay invested in the company; it shows confidence and trust, and it saves them on the final payout. We always maintained that, with respect to equity, we would either hold a majority so we controlled our asset or a significant minority so that the investment would not be a material part of our personal assets' portfolio. We kept 10% of our equity as an investment with the new firm, something that paid off incredibly well 2.5 years later when PE sold the entire company to a global consulting firm in October 2021. We got our "second bite of the apple", and there would not be a third bite.

PREPARING YOUR PERSONAL ESTATE
FOR AN EXIT

Trusts

OK, so your company is ready for an exit, you have a mature executive and management team, valuable contracts, a plan for the team, and a realistic idea of the value . . . now let's do a transaction!

Not so fast; there is planning to do on the personal side as well. Too many times we heard stories about founders who were so busy with their companies that their personal estate planning never happened; suddenly, they are faced with an imminent transaction, and they want things to be set in place in a hurry. This is clearly a mistake. Ask around for an estate attorney and/or a wealth manager, someone who can build a personal strategy for you and your family. We urge founders to not wait too long; often procrastination happens because they don't think that they need wealth management. Believe us, we didn't either, until we did, and then we were grateful that we had everything planned and ready. It takes time to talk to multiple people until you find someone you are comfortable with, and estate planning can be confusing if you're not familiar with it, and most people are not, we know we weren't.

This book is not an estate planning guide, and we are not the experts you should be taking advice from, other than the advice to begin this process early, before your company has significant value. There are time-consuming activities involved, such as a company valuation (remember from earlier in this chapter), to establish a basis for gift tax purposes, the creation of trusts, and more.

By coincidence, we already had a long-term relationship with a savvy and experienced estate attorney. This began many years pre-Dovel when Elma was not yet a U.S. citizen. Dov was listening to a radio program in which this attorney was talking about estate planning, and he learned that, should he pass away, passing marital assets to Elma, as a non-US citizen, would be a taxable event. We established a relationship with this estate attorney that lasted for more than 25 years.

As our company/personal portfolio grew in value and complexity, we grew the team by including a global wealth advisory team, an accounting and tax team, and legal advisors. We met multiple times to develop a post-transaction, as well as a post–Dov and Elma (we are very pragmatic and realistic people. . .), strategy based on our values, a strategy that would work for our family for generations to come. Think of it as investing in the well-being of your family for multiple generations.

It takes time to build a team, develop a strategy, and understand what your values are and what you want your legacy to be. We admit that our strategy changed over time, as we became more informed, and more comfortable, with the various options, IRS guidelines, and tax laws.

Donor-Advised Fund

A major part of the strategy and planning evolves around values, and for us, one of our core values is education. We believe that education is ultimately what brought us success, and we also believe that a sound education allows people to support themselves, determine their own destiny, and become informed citizens of a society. With that in mind, we support students through scholarships and savings plans for kids in our circles. An estate planning tool we use for some of this is the donor-advised fund (DAF), which is like a foundation but with different guidelines. Deciding on distributions from our DAF is an annual family activity that brings multiple generations around the table to talk about their values and what to support.

In Summary

A corporate transaction might very well be the most impactful event in your personal, professional, and financial life. Preparing for this will save you from frustration, aggravation, and anxiety and help you avoid costly mistakes and regrets.

11

ENTREPRENEURSHIP ADVICE FOR ALL

From College Students to Experienced Founders

We regularly present workshops for start-up founders, give talks at business and engineering schools, and speak at tech and industry conferences. We get many questions, and they are in three broad categories:

- Starting and scaling a company
- Transaction (including what planning should be done on the company side and on the personal side 2 years before transaction)
- The impact of running a company as a couple – Should we do it together?

So, in this chapter, we provide all the wisdom that we accumulated.

DOI: 10.4324/9781003260653-13

If you arrived at this chapter by reading all the previous chapters (and didn't jump directly to it), you've read our story, you've read about how Dovel Technologies started and ended, and you may understand who we are, how we got here, and what it took to get here.

Malcolm Gladwell, in his book *Outliers*, writes:

> Success is not a random act. It arises out of a predictable and powerful set of circumstances and opportunities.[1]

And we know that this is so true; it took opportunity, preparation, luck, and much more to get to where we are. In general, we have a positive outlook on life; we believe that it makes it simpler to handle life's ups and downs if we look for the silver linings and the "good" that came out of a challenging time. We also are risk-takers and adventurers, always ready to take on a new "thing", overcome a new challenge, and learn something different. "Bring it on" and "what's the worst that can happen" are our approaches in our business lives as well as in personal lives, as you will see in the chapter about our travel. A "can-do" attitude and a positive outlook impacts everything you do because it shapes how you see what's in front of you and how you experience challenges, and that, in turn, impacts the decisions you make. We believe that your life's attitude significantly determines your success as an entrepreneur.

Current events in the U.S., as well as worldwide, can cause you to feel fearful for the future of our children's and our children's children; however, our involvements with young ambitious, smart, and innovative students at several universities, and young ambitious leaders of start-up firms show us that the future is bright, and the creative ideas are flourishing. Many students we speak to are interested in becoming entrepreneurs and we think that's great. All we advise is that you get some work experience as an employee and that do your homework: are you ready for the unknowns? Do you have a viable idea on which to build a business model? Is there a true need for your solution? It's not enough that you think it has great value to the universe because you will not be your customer; do your customer discovery and find out what the research tells you.

Elma

Once Paul took over, and I was no longer actively involved in operations at Dovel, I served as a mentor and advisor to entrepreneurs and start-up business owners for the School of Entrepreneurship at George Washington University, as well as for SCORE, a nonprofit national organization supporting business owners, and the National Science Foundation (NSF) ICORPS program. I was not only very impressed with the smart, ambitious, and innovative minds and the creative ideas, but I also witnessed some situations of concern:

- Founder(s) too impressed with their own idea/solution/product to objectively assess market need
- Founder(s) too focused with getting funding and sharing too much equity
- Founder(s) being too impressed with "experts" who want to be part of the endeavor, without assessing if this is a healthy and productive partnership
- Founder(s) who believe that the "trappings" are more important than the quality of the product/solution they sell, or the revenues, or the customer

I could go on, but you get the idea. It behooves you to think it through, do your homework, focus on what's important, and get a mentor who you trust. I really like the mentoring work and realized that I had a lot to share, much of it was wisdom gained in hindsight, but wisdom nonetheless, so I completed a leadership coaching program at George Mason University; set up my coaching practice, Coach to Strength, LLC; and now work with business leaders. I love the work, and I am in awe of my clients' wisdom, maturity, and leadership skills.

I thought long and hard about the name of my coaching venture, and it's unusual, I admit, but I had concluded that "strength and resilience" are foundational to success in both life and business. This is probably a subject for another book, but in short, strength and resilience got us through many difficult times, both personal as well as professional; a strong and resilient governance infrastructure was foundational to the successful strategy change at Dovel; strong personal and corporate financials enabled us to take on risky efforts, like the Laboratory Information Management System (LIMS) proposal, and a strong and resilient relationship allowed us to build the American dream together and celebrate 40 years of marriage in 2022. We raised our children, Mark and Karyn, to be strong, resilient, and independent, because we believe that that's the foundation for a happy and successful life; seeing them as successful strong young adults building their lives in their own way makes us proud beyond words.

Entrepreneurs must be leaders, visionaries, trailblazers, and the optimists of the organization. I must admit that I learned this lesson late: when you are a corporate leader, people look to what you do *and* what you don't do, what you say, how you say it, and what you don't say; you lead by example, and you're being watched; your reactions and responses are weighted and measured. This is a lot of responsibility, but it goes with the territory. It's also a lonely place, and trusted mentors and friends are critical. A trusted friend/mentor will tell you what you need to hear, not what you want to hear, and they will not share what you've told them with anyone. For me, my friend Linda was, and still is, my trusted support. As an entrepreneur and business owner, who built and sold her business, she understood my challenges and gave me support when needed. My wish for all you entrepreneurs, leaders, founders, and creative innovators is that you find a friend and mentor to support you.

Regarding business partnerships, those are like marriages; many go wrong because of differences of opinion around strategy, expectations, and money. Be careful who you decide to go into partnership with. Just because you've been best friends since childhood doesn't mean that you can be in a business partnership; during my time as a mentor, I've seen business partnership friendships come apart, and it's sad when that happens. Think to yourself, "Do I really need a business partner? Perhaps I can hire the skillsets that I need to complement mine?" Talk it over with your mentor/coach!

Know Your Strengths!

One more very important piece of advice before I "hand the pen" back over to Dov: know yourself and know what you do best; in other words, *Know Your Strengths*! If I had to name one decision I made for the company that was both the hardest for me and the best for the company, it was knowing when it was time to bring in another skill set, get out of the way, and let Paul take Dovel to the next level. I wrote about this in the chapter on letting go (Chapter 9); I knew it was the right thing to do, I knew it was the best for Dovel, for the team, and, ultimately, for Dov and me. I knew all that, but it was still difficult. I chose to look at it in a positive way, however; rather than allowing my ego to get all bruised and twisted, I recognized what my strengths were: creating something out of nothing, organizing and putting structure in place, building a strong yet flexible foundation for growth, and fostering a warm and inclusive culture, and that those strengths were most needed in the start-up and early growth phase.

I was once in the audience of a panel conversation. The panelists were angel investors, entrepreneurs, and a few others. I clearly recall the answer of the angel investor to a question from the audience: "What are you looking for in a leader for the companies in your portfolio?" His reply: "Someone with the right strengths for the right phase of the company". This stayed with me. . .

So, to the founders/entrepreneurs/leaders among you, know your strengths and recognize when you need to bring in different skill sets; it may just be the best thing you do for your company, for your team and for yourself.

Dov

Elma occasionally refers to a famous poem by Robert Frost, called "The Road not Taken", asking, "What would have happened if . . ." Obviously, as someone with a more left-brain approach, I immediately reject the mere notion of second-guessing. It is impossible to look at every decision we made and ask ourselves if another decision would have been wiser. So since we are unable to say with any degree of certainty that, at a certain point, we should have done something different, we might as well try to explain our decisions. We don't know if these were the best decisions, but one thing we know: it is better to make the "wrong" decision than not deciding at all and let circumstances take you by default. Elma also likes to say, "Live by design and not by default"; in other words, be decisive, don't led events just happen, stay in the driver's seat, and move forward.

We have met many successful entrepreneurs as well as many "wannabee" entrepreneurs, and we wrote earlier about the ingredients to make it all work: preparedness, opportunity, luck, focus, and more. Let's add to that the following: How valid is (a) *your business idea and your willingness to pivot*, (b) *your network and your support system*, and (c) *your level of perseverance and resilience*? Let's look at each one as they pertain to you, the aspiring entrepreneur. Reminder again, this is based on *our* experience, and it does not hold a promise, nor a threat, for your story.

a. Your business idea and your willingness to pivot

The common advice from mentors is to write a 3- to 5-year business plan.

Elma: As a business mentor I often asked that my aspiring entrepreneurial clients write a short 3- to 5-page business plan. The plan document itself was not the most important; the reason behind this assignment was to gauge the client's ability to really think things through and articulate their strategy by writing it down. There would be two main groups of clients: one group would not come back or would come back with ideas but never write a plan, and another group would obsess over every paragraph of the plan, unable to focus and articulate their ideas. Only some clients would come with a coherent plan, and ready to execute. Same idea behind writing your mission statement, a 1- to 3-sentence statement that articulates what your company's purpose is. It's a lot harder to do than you think. Go to several company websites and read the mission and vision statements, a lot of words not saying much, and in general, all use similar language.

Articulating your mission, vision, and business plan is hard, and that's why it's an important early exercise. I wrote in an earlier chapter about how I got to write the mission and vision, I admit that I did not think it to be important at the time, but I remember that it wasn't easy to do, and in hindsight, like so much of the Dovel journey, it was an important exercise.

One more important aspect of your business idea. I learned this when I served twice as a team mentor for the National Science Foundation's (NSF's) Innovation Corps (ICORPS) program. The objective behind this national program is to encourage innovating entrepreneurs to go "out of the building" to validate their business idea. This program was created because so many start-ups fail in the first 1 to 3 years as a result of the founders building something that nobody wanted to buy. Based on that valuable experience, my advice is that you do your market research in an objective manner with a very open mind: ask open-ended questions, hear what they say, not what you want to hear, and be open to pivoting. Avoid confirmation bias, and the arrogance of thinking that you just need to "educate the customer". Let me share a brief made-up story to illustrate this:

Innovative do-gooders come to a village and see the women walking every morning with buckets and containers to collect water from the common well. This looks hard and time-consuming, so the do-gooders devise a system to get fresh water to each home in the village. Despite completion of this system, they observe that the women continue their daily ritual of walking to the well to collect water. The reason: the well gave the women a valid reason to meet every morning and socialize; this was important to them. The innovators had decided what the value proposition was without asking the women!

Advice to entrepreneurs: don't assume that you know what the value proposition of your business idea is: "Ask the women!" and keep an open mind to pivot when needed.

Dov: We did not write a business plan, but if we had, it would make no mention of the federal information technology (IT) market as that did not look like an attractive place to do business and we did not have any experience in that market. My first three jobs were commercial, and Integrated Data Corporation (IDC)/Dovel's first customer CompuMark U.S., was a privately held commercial company. However, when opportunity knocked in the form of a phone call from a previous employer and friend calling me about EDGAR, I didn't say, "We are not doing government work"; instead, I listened to what they had to say, liked the opportunity, and thus, IDC/Dovel became a government contracting company. This worked because we were still in the very early start-up phase, developing a viable business model. That's the time when an objective mind, and a willingness to pivot, is most important. Over time, there must be a balance between focusing on your market and your solution and pivoting as the landscape changes. My initial negative thoughts about the federal market were based on nothing more than subjective hearsay, and I am glad I kept an open mind when opportunity knocked.

Here's another example of an unexpected "left-field curveball" opportunity that would never have been in our "never-written" business plan.

During my time as a technical architect for a large BDM program at the American Red Cross (ARC), I happened to be in a conversation with the project manager and learn of corporate's frustration with managing the multiple subcontractors I had brought on to supplement the BDM employees and ensure a successful team. He suggested, "Why don't they submit the timesheets and invoices to IDC/Dovel, and then you submit one consolidated invoice? You can add a handling fee". Now remember that, as a technical person, taking on this administrative hassle was not at all anywhere in my plan of building an IT company, so I could have said, "Nice, but no thank you . . . don't need this headache at this time in my life". But I recognized the opportunity and said, "Sure". Until that time, the revenues came from my billable hours, 1 hour at the time, but with this addition, every hour was worth so much more. By reinvesting the 5% handling fee into the company, we had the fuel for the initial growth. As the administrative burden grew and other opportunities happened, Elma took over, organizing and developing the corporate governance structure, and the rest is history. Lesson Learned: when a door opens, walk through it to see what is on the other side; what's the worst that can happen?

b. Your network and your support system

We've discussed at length the importance of relationships and networking in previous chapters, so not much left to add; however, we want to bring it up again in this chapter because your network is so critical to your success. We're not just talking about attending a gazillion networking events, making hundreds of small-talk convos, and collecting dozens of business cards; these activities are important and necessary, but these by themselves do not create your network and support system. It takes time and commitment to bring people into your circle of trust and to learn to give and take. A supportive relationship must be a win–win, and we have been so very fortunate to reap the personal and professional benefits of long-term relationships: our advisory board was made up of people with whom we had stayed connected, we knew and trusted Paul to become our CEO because we knew each other from back then, Elma met Linda at a networking event and had cultivated a mutually supportive friendship, and on and on. There is one example we reinforce, especially to the younger aspiring entrepreneurs among you: don't be too timid to reach out and connect with the more established people you meet.

Elma: I participate frequently on speaking panels, and usually the last question to the panelists is to give their parting advice; my advice: *be bold and ask one of us for coffee!* I have met multiple people who have done just that and still have relationships with some. We had the same experience with students as we speak at universities, and we leave our business cards and invite students to contact us directly; we still have relationships with some who took us up on it. When I was in the audience when Linda was on a panel, I was bold, asked her for coffee ("believe me, I was nervous, but what's the worst that could happen"), and the rest is history.

Not everyone in your network becomes your support system, but you will only know by building and developing your relationships. We will emphasize this again and again!

c. Your level of perseverance and resilience

Here's what we hear from some entrepreneurial wannabees: I want to start my own business so I can make my own hours . . . well, where to begin with this. . .

As soon as the company has additional employees, and especially when overhead staff needs to be supported, the pressure is on to not only maintain the revenue stream but also to increase it. This means ensuring performance quality, feeding the business development pipeline, providing opportunities to the team, and on and on and on.

All this comes on the shoulders of the founder(s), who, especially in the beginning, also may have operational and/or program responsibilities on one or more customer-facing programs. There usually aren't enough hours in the day, or week, to accomplish it all. As the company grows the pressure grows, to us it felt like we were on a treadmill that kept increasing speed: no time to slow down and add support staff to take the load of, can't get off without the whole thing collapsing, just have to keep going. The feeling of always coming up short extends to your family life. For us, it was the norm to continue our work after having dinner with the kids. Every evening was spent in front of the computer, catching up on things for which there wasn't any time during the day. It takes its toll, and without perseverance and resilience, it gets very hard to sustain. In the very beginning, when Dov had a business partner, this partner's wife asked me, "Will my husband have to work as hard as Dov?" I told Dov that this wasn't going to be a good business partnership because his business partner did not have his family's support, and it would take more perseverance and resilience than he and his wife had. The partnership soon collapsed.

A successful ending, like the Dovel story has, may mask the sweat, tears, and energy it took to make it all work. It hurts to look back and know that our children did not always get our full attention, and there are regrets about often being "too busy" to spend time with ageing parents.

So it would be great to make my own hours? Go on vacation whenever I want? Be my own boss? Go into it with your eyes wide open, talk to experienced business owners, and be honest with yourself, your life partner, and your business partner.

Note

1   Gladwell Malcolm. Outliers: *The Story of Success*. Little, Brown and Company; Hachette Book Group, 2008, Kindle, Web. 12 January 2021.

12

WHY TRAVEL ADVENTURES?

This isn't a travel book, even though we would enjoy writing such a book. So, you might ask yourself, why do I see a chapter about travel adventures in this book. To Elma and me, there is a good explanation, so, keep on reading.

DOI: 10.4324/9781003260653-14

During the early Dovel years, when our children were still young, we traveled mostly to our native countries, Israel and The Netherlands, to visit our families. After all, we couldn't take much time off, and with the time that we had, we wanted to make sure that our children got to know their family and heritage. Several times Elma suggested camping, but it wasn't for Dov, who used the excuse of his army years and how he still remembers having to "shave with cold water" to avoid this "suffering". The truth is that, even on vacation, we couldn't completely disconnect from our company, and things always seemed to wait for when we were gone to go haywire. We recall an event in which we received a call about an administrative matter while on top of a remote mountain in Iceland.

As we scaled and brought in more staff, the company began to run itself without our constant presence, so it gave us a little more opportunity to getaway. We took multiple family trips with the kids to the Bahamas, Caymans, Arizona, and other places, where we always did something new as a family: get diving certifications, go ATV'ing in the desert, and hiking up Mount Masada to watch the sun coming up over the Dead Sea. For this, the kids, ages 11 and 13 at the time, complained the entire way up, but we insisted because we were confident that, one day, they would talk about it with gratitude (we're still waiting, but soon now. . .). We always tried to go just outside our comfort zones and provide Mark and Karyn with opportunities to grow and learn something new. Mark went to multiple adventure summer camps, and Karyn got her sailing certificates during summer camps. We wanted them to gain confidence by experiencing new challenges and learn that they can adjust and overcome to be resilient and strong.

You might ask yourself, "Why do I see a chapter on their travel adventures? How does this relate to their business story?" There is a relationship: by now you've recognized that building a company, especially as a married couple, is very demanding. It's a 24/7 all-encompassing involvement. However, life requires some time to take a step back and think about the business. We found that our adventure hiking travel helped us accomplish that and more:

- It requires significant planning, thus taking our mind from Dovel for some hours at a time during the planning phase.
- It helped us stay in strong physical shape – staying in shape when you work many hours is at the same time critically important and challenging as there is always a reason why you do not have time to exercise and to eat right. But if you plan to go on a strenuous hike in 6 months, you have a good reason to maintain your weight and stay in good shape. Your reward is the adventure.
- It provided time off – as we all know, we are living in a connected world. In today's world, when we are all connected to our smartphones, it is impossible to escape from telephone calls, voice mails, emails, texts, WhatsApp, Facebook, and on and on. Thus, even the best vacation does not provide any separation from work. However, on adventure travel with either spotty or no cell phone connection, you are disconnected from work.
- You discover and challenge your risk tolerance. For example, climbing Mount Kilimanjaro requires taking risks, but you can manage these risks in the same way that you can manage the risks at your company: planning, listening to more experienced people who have done what you're going to do, getting physically and mentally ready, prepare for the worst, and get ready.

So, maybe, as you will read later, we fell into adventure travel/hiking by coincidence, but we found out that we very much enjoy it, and we are continuing it now in the post-Dovel days.

We hope that you, the reader, will find something of interest that will allow you to find time away from the company, and maybe, just maybe, you will fall in love with adventure travel.

Part III

EPILOGUE

13

THE FINAL CHAPTER

After we concluded the transaction with the private equity firm in May 2019, Dovel continued to grow, both organically and via acquisitions. Elma and I were proud to see the Dovel logo on our building. However, we were wondering how the story would end . . .

DOI: 10.4324/9781003260653-16

Figure 13.1 Dovel ACG Award 2021

On Saturday, September 4, 2021, Veritas Capital–backed Guide-house acquired Dovel Technologies.[1]

This was the conclusion of a journey that began in 2000 with Dov and Elma, followed by the very impactful involvement of Paul in 2011, and the "recap" by McQuarrie in 2019.

We were surprised at how quickly the final transaction happened – especially compared to the previous one, in which we were much more involved. We learned of ongoing discussions over the summer, received a call about the successful conclusion one weekend in September, and the closing was 3 days later, which was followed by many press releases: this was a story in the government contracting world!

On the day of closing, Damon Griggs, Dovel's CEO, accepted an award and gave an emotional speech on behalf of Dovel Technologies. Dovel went out with a bang!!

For us, this was a bittersweet event because, unlike the previous transaction in 2019, Dovel would be merged into a large global firm, and the company would lose its name and identity. Also, this transaction ended our involvement as equity stakeholders, and the signage, with the logo that our sister designed, will come off the buildings.

For us, after three acquisitions and two transactions, we've come full circle. We feel good about the outcome, but, mostly, we feel good about the impact our company has had, and continues to have, on so many people: financially, professionally, and personally.

This final transaction will significantly simplify our lives, especially with respect to the many state tax returns, the various non-compete agreements, and even the fact that many people would still reach out to us because they assumed that we continued to have influence in the company.

This transaction caused us to reflect on what we started: initially with Integrated Data Corporation, which led to the Dovel story.

We remember coming to the U.S. 40 years ago as two young, poor, and naive students from The Netherlands and Israel. Over time, we both received our master's degrees; started a company that, with the help of an incredible team, grew into a significant player in the industry; successfully sold the company; have two wonderful kids and an amazing granddaughter; and are still very much a team together. This is a fantastic journey, and we are proud of it.

Figure 13.2 Dovel's CEOs
From left: Dov (1st CEO), Elma (2nd CEO), Damon (4th CEO), and
Paul (3rd CEO) at the 2021 GovCon (Greater Washington Government
Contractor) Awards™ Gala
This event closed the Dovel journey.

Was it worth it? We both will say yes, mainly because of the
positive impact we had on so many people's lives.

What will we do next? Only time will tell, but in addition to
investing in early-stage start-ups via our Eldov Group company,
I am sure that we won't sit idle. Our future will involve giving back
by supporting education, innovation, and entrepreneurship, with
resources as well as time and guidance.

Note

1   www.businesswire.com/news/home/20210908005514/en/
Guidehouse-to-Acquire-Dovel-Technologies

14

THE WORLD POST-COVID-19

Trends We're Following

After the Dovel transaction in 2019, we established the Eldov Group, LLC (from Dovel to Eldov – how creative) our boutique investment and start-up advisory company. Our early-stage start-up investments are companies with solutions that are at the intersection between health care (Elma's background) and information technology (IT; Dov's background.)

As we all observed during, and probably because of, the pandemic, many people left the workforce and started new businesses. We hope this chapter will be helpful to readers who are looking for start-up ideas and trends, as well as start-up entrepreneurs.

DOI: 10.4324/9781003260653-17

Dov

In late 2019, in the world before COVID-19, Elma and I established Eldov Group with the "objective of investing in early start-up companies as well as fueling organic growth in areas such as biomedical informatics, scientific research and development, advanced analytics, cloud computing, Machine Learning, Artificial Intelligence, security, and more . . ."

The name "Eldov" gives Elma the credit she deserves with her name first. It was funny when we told one of our attorneys about the name we chose for the new company, he said: "Dov, everybody always knew who was first". It brought a smile to my face.

This new endeavor allows us to not only help some companies financially but with other support, guidance, introductions, and the like, as well. With our selection criteria, we concentrate on what's important to both of us: IT, public health, and leadership. Since we maintained excellent relationships with people in Israel who are in the venture capital, health care, and IT industries, and since Israel is known as the "start-up country", we decided to start there and move to start-ups in our backyard, the U.S., later.

In January 2020, we went to Israel to meet with several entrepreneurial founders and invested in two companies. We continued our Israel National Trail hike in the Negev Desert for fun, something we do for several days every time we go to Israel. Little did we know then that COVID-19 would shut down our travel for at least 2 years.

Later that month, January 27, 2020, we became grandparents for the first time . . . what an experience! Unfortunately, our daughter and son-in-law live near Seattle, so we were able to hold our sweet granddaughter, Isabelle, only twice, at age 3 days and 3 weeks, before lockdowns prevented us from holding her in our arms again until she was 14 months old. It made us very sad, but fortunately, we were in an excellent situation with housing and income security for all our loved ones; we recognize that many people were not so fortunate.

COVID-Related Transformation of the Workplace

On the professional side, as a consultant to the GrantSolutions program, I noticed the impact of the pandemic almost overnight: there was a significant increase in the number of grants, all work became telework, causing lots of empty commercial real estate and remote work technologies flourishing.

The GrantSolutions program's mission is to manage and oversee billions of dollars' worth of grants annually for the federal government; on average, pre-COVID, this would be about $50 to $70 billion; however, as we closed fiscal year 2021, GrantSolutions processed more than $200 billion worth of grants. A significant portion of it is for COVID-19-related grants that had to be awarded quickly. A serious challenge of a significant increase in work volume while adjusting to the remote work situation. Nobody would have thought that this was going to be successful or even feasible.

A full-floor full-scale office renovation of our space was completed in January 2020! A beautiful space with lots of areas for teams to sit together and collaborate, a social "hang-out" place for lunch, and, of course, the Friday breakfast and more. Enough to energize and motivate more than 200 people to work together and be creative and productive. This became "yesterday's thinking" before it had a chance to start, as everyone was forced to work remotely as of early March, and things were never the same and probably will never be the same.

Remote Knowledge Worker

If you would have asked me pre-pandemic if we could transition, almost overnight, a few hundred people from working in the office to working remotely successfully while managing a doubling workload, I am sure my response would have been: "We need to look into it, plan the transition, do a pilot, learn from the pilot and phase it in carefully, over time" But in the Spring of 2020, we didn't have the luxury of time, and, interestingly enough, it all it worked above expectation. Across the IT industry, we hear about increased productivity, improved work-life balance, and overall work satisfaction. Of course, people struggled, especially parents with young and school-aged children. Still, overall, people made it work and developed a renewed appreciation for family, work mission, and personal well-being. Tools were created and improved to address the inevitable technical issues, and people adjusted. COVID-19 accelerated a change that had already begun but had been met hesitation and skepticism from the more traditional leaders. Mitigation measures of the pandemic created a megatrend that shaped people's lives and organizations' workflows and growth and productivity strategies. Overall, people didn't enjoy the lockdown, but the remote work situation brought pleasures that weren't there before: no commute, a more relaxed work atmosphere, and more balanced lives. So, concerning working remotely, we learned that not only can it be done, but it also has significant benefits!

Remote work has extended into other industries as well, work that used to be so totally person-to-person oriented that virtual was unthinkable: who would have thought that doctors' appointments could be virtual and would be reimbursable by insurance! That virtual coaching and therapy sessions would turn out to be very effective; some even say that they are more effective as there are fewer "no-shows" or frazzled clients caused by commutes, transportation costs, and limited parking. Elma, in her coaching practice, works with several clients whom she has never met in person, and the coach–client relationship is solid and impactful.

Since this is not a mature market, there are many areas where things can improve. For example, a few years ago, did we ever think that Zoom/Microsoft Teams would become such an essential part of our lives?

Vacant Commercial Real Estate

If you walk downtown of any major city, you hear mostly quiet. When you assess the various activities near these office buildings, you will see a significant decline in business activities. Restaurants, convenient stores, dry cleaning, and office cleaning are suffering. We are starting to hear about creative solutions such as converting offices to apartment buildings or taking the space and creating incubators for a start-up zone and thus changing the look of a typical downtown to encourage the vibrancy of the major American cities. Only time will tell in which direction this trend will continue to evolve.

So is there an opportunity for start-ups to benefit from this trend? Someone is going to come up with innovative ideas about what to do with the space, how to design the as-is to the to-be, and definitely how to implement it. There are always winners and losers, and there will be start-ups that will seize the opportunities.

Technologies

Concerning technologies, there has been an acceleration of innovation in part due to the pandemic allowing many start-ups to improve the remote worker lifestyle: for example, the ability for remote teams to work together, harmoniously, all toward a common goal, significantly improved since March of 2020 and will undoubtedly continue to evolve.

- **Cloud computing:** the on-demand availability of computer system resources, like data storage and computing power, without direct user interaction.
- **Artificial intelligence (AI):** the ability of a computer to learn by using data
- **Machine learning (ML):** a component of AI, the ability of a computer to learn and create predictive algorithms based on data
- **Low-code/no-code platforms:** these platforms provide for a simple and fast alternative to traditional development processes, allowing founders/entrepreneurs with no formal coding skills to meet their business demands to develop an app, automate processes, and boost digital transformation. In 2021, in response to COVID-19, we had to establish a way to

release money quickly, we built some capability using a low code/no-code platform and made it available very quickly.

There are definitely significant opportunities for start-ups in the area of AI and ML, as we have observed over the past few years. Now that so much business is conducted remotely, ML and AI make significant improvements possible, and the pace is only accelerating.

Health Care

COVID-19 exposed some significant weaknesses in our health care system, and sure enough, the conversation about how to fix the system has heated up again. Health care in the U.S. is a complicated subject. As immigrants, we have a unique understanding of several other health care systems in the world, and we are always surprised to hear our U.S. system being compared to that of a small European country like Denmark or Sweden or Canada. And often, the comparison comes with incorrect assumptions and beliefs. Indeed, like our son, Mark, would say, "If we could redesign the U.S. health care system, no one would come up with what we have". However, we have what we have, and we can use technology to improve on it.

It doesn't take a genius to see that the trajectory of the health care expenditure as a percentage of gross domestic product is unsustainable as we move into the future and as people live longer. One of the measures to mitigate spiraling cost is the trend toward value-based health care, in which provider organizations are paid a set amount for a geographic cohort that incentivizes the provider to keep the people healthy and out of institutionalized care. This, in turn, has caused a significant increase in interest in public health–related solutions, which is facilitated by the increased availability of the newer technologies, such as ML, AI, cloud technologies, and computing in general. There are many start-ups using these technologies to build solutions that benefit public health by increasing independent living and improving quality of life. Through our new venture, the Eldov Group, we are investors in several start-ups that all focus on building these types of solutions and find it very exciting and rewarding to play a part in this.

Security

Due to increased virtual work, as well as other, less noble, opportunistic activities caused, in part, by the isolation of lockdowns, the security of the internet severely deteriorated during the pandemic. We all receive daily, if not more frequent, reminders of the fragility of the security of our virtual presence impacting our businesses as well as our personal lives. The threat has become much more sophisticated; whereas hackers used to be able to get to our information by compromising our computer, we see more and more that large companies are being compromised and that hundreds of thousands of accounts are being sold on the dark web. How does this impact a start-up? As you focus on building your company and developing a solution, you increasingly have to spend valuable resources on securing the infrastructure and ensuring that your company is on solid ground. Failing to recognize this can cost you dearly.

When will we see the end of the oversized role COVID-19 plays in our lives? Only time will tell; there have been many predictions, but those are often true only in hindsight. We hope the world will be a different place by the time you read this book. One thing is sure, however; whenever we are on the other side of the pandemic, we will have learned a lot (we hope): work lives and personal lives will look different, our expectations and values will have adjusted, and the world will look different than it did before March 2020. Despite all the pain, sickness, and death experienced by too many, there are silver linings . . . if only you remember and know where to look for them.

15

OUR TRAVEL ADVENTURES

Why are we adding a chapter about our travel adventures? Because, as you will read, our hiking adventures were a significant part of our story, both during and after Dovel, we have learned that *Solvitur Ambulando* ("it is solved by walking") is very accurate, as it provides a way to disengage completely. The adventure also requires commitment, planning, risk tolerance, resilience, and trust in each other . . . you see the parallels? We hope you enjoy this chapter, and, who knows, perhaps it will inspire you.

DOI: 10.4324/9781003260653-18

Solvitur Ambulando ("it is solved by walking")

We described earlier in the book the benefits that adventure travel can provide entrepreneurs and why we chose it as a way to relieve the pressure and enable totally disconnecting.

We also strongly believe there is a significant correlation between the risks you are willing to take as an entrepreneur and the risk you are willing to take in your adventure travel, and it may lead to some discussion about risk tolerance.

Over the years, we have received many questions regarding adventure travel and how to get started. So, just to get you interested, we wanted to describe some trips. We thought long and hard about which one we should include and decided to write about two of our most favorite: the very first trip to the Grand Canyon and summiting Mount Kilimanjaro. Our goal is not to say, "Look what we have accomplished", instead, we hope that this will help you decide if this is for you.

Since that time, we have hiked in many parts of the world and have done some other travel adventures around the world. We know we're fortunate that we both crave adventure and excitement, no "sitting on the beach" vacations for us yet. We visited the gorillas in Uganda and the grizzlies in Alaska. We traversed the infamous Drake Passage and jumped in the ice-cold polar water in Antarctica, holding hands as we went under. But the hiking trips continue to give us the most fun, challenge, and benefit since these trips force us to stay in shape and plan as a team. We hiked the Alta Via, an 11-day hut-to-hut hike in northern Italy, the 4-day Machu Pichu trail, the W in Patagonia, and the biggest of all: Kilimanjaro. It is only because of COVID-19 that we have not yet conquered, the Amalfi Coast, and Everest Basecamp, but there is still time.

2008: The Grand Canyon

In the spring of 2008, for Elma's 50th birthday, our friends, who are both avid hikers, invited us to come with them in November of that year, and hike the Grand Canyon, stay overnight in Phantom Ranch, and hike back up. Elma was very excited about this opportunity, but I was skeptical; after all, we had never hiked in our life. I asked, "There are mules, right? Why not take the mules down?" but I quickly realized that Elma was going with or without me, and I was either going to join her or be left behind. So, after thinking it over for an hour or so, I said, "If we want to do it, we better prepare for it". We bought equipment and began going on day hikes in Shenandoah National Park. We were ready when the time came, and we truly enjoyed trekking down the South Kaibab trail to Phantom Ranch. Soon, I knew exactly what to expect and what the path looked like. The good news was that an hour into the hike, there was no reception. No more e-mails, calls or voice mails. It was liberating, and we knew that until we reached roughly the same elevation on the way up, no more Dovel on our mind as we needed to concentrate on our hike.

That first night at the Phantom Ranch, I saw the full moon lighting up the Grand Canyon as if it was the middle of the day. It reminded me of my army days in the Sinai Desert (anyone who has seen a full moon in the desert or snow recognizes what I am talking about). I told Elma that these are the perfect conditions to hike at night. At dinner the next day, I asked a staff member, "If your shift ended today, would you climb up tonight", and she responded, "There aren't as many days as perfect as today, perfect temperature, too cold for snakes". I wasn't sure how Elma would take it, and our friends had already declined an invitation to hike up at night, when I suddenly overheard someone at our communal table ask Elma, "So, are you and Dov going to hike up tonight?" to which she replied, "Sure!" I was astonished. After dinner, we bought two tiny flashlights and got on our way; at 7 p.m., the moon had not yet risen over the mountains, so the valley was pitch black. It was scary until the moon was high enough to light up the canyon. The night climb was cold and magical. Elma and I felt like we were alone in the world. We didn't encounter snakes or dangerous animals, just one herd of mule deer standing on the narrow path, preventing us from passing. We stared at them, and they at us; we threw a few rocks at their feet, and they fled. The hike was a 7.5-hour continuous trek up, with no breaks because it was too cold to stop moving. Around 2:30 a.m., we arrived at the rim. A parking lot night guard watched us come up in amazement. "Where are you coming from?" he asked. "Phantom Ranch", we said as if this was a daily occurrence. He looked at us as if we were crazy.

Elma: the first few hours, when it was very dark, and after the first of our two flashlights had already given out, I was nervous. I heard all kinds of noises, and I was very concerned that Dov would trip over a rock or something and fall over the edge. Without any cellphone connectivity, what would I do if that happened? It never occurred to me that the same could happen to me.

Then, and I recall this moment, I said to myself: "Stop it! This is a once-in-a-lifetime experience, and you're ruining it by being scared instead of enjoying the moment. What's the worst that can happen?" As usual, it worked. I enjoyed the adventure. The stars were like diamonds in the sky, and it felt as if we owned the Grand Canyon that night. And nothing terrible happened.

That year was the same time my father passed away, and there was a lot of painful and stressful tension in the company and between us. Our hiking adventure was like therapy, and I learned that the axiom *Solvitur Ambulando* is very true.

Summiting the Kilimanjaro

I remember searching for a new adventure when I came across stories about Mount Kilimanjaro. By that time, we knew how to plan and execute a complex hiking trip. So, one day I suggested to Elma that we tackle this, and she agreed.

Once we put this on the radar, we had to do lots of research and physical preparation. To summit Mount Kilimanjaro, we had to find a tour company, as it is not allowed to hike up the mountain without a certified guide. As with everything else we do, when we take on a challenge, we embrace it and enjoy it to the fullest. We watched YouTube videos, read everything possible, and researched what we were going to need. We knew that the last night, as we would reach 19,341 feet elevation, it would be freezing, and the air would be thin. We knew we better plan for it as on that final climbing night, we had seven layers of clothing on top and four layers on the bottom, and we needed to be able to walk for many hours in the dark and in a low oxygen environment.

We talked about possible scenarios, such as what to do if one of us couldn't continue. We decided that, if this is due to low oxygen levels, the nonimpacted person will continue, since the impacted person would have a guide with them taking them to lower altitudes, where the problem would be immediately solved. However, if either of us cannot continue for any other reason, we stay together. Luckily, nothing happened, and we both made it to the summit.

Climbing Mount Kilimanjaro was a very challenging adventure, both mental as well as physical. Over time the altitude was noticeable, and we began to feel weaker. Our appetite declined, and the guide watched closely that we, our group of eight, ate and drank

Figure 15.1 Elma and Dov took Dovel to the top of the Kilimanjaro

enough. The nights were freezing, and after a full day of hiking, there was only a little finger bowl with water to clean up. After eight days and nights, we completed this adventure and we were back on a plane home, but it took several more days for our bodies to "heal".

The Dovel team was very much with us on this trip; everyone was so excited that we both made it to the summit. We brought a SPOT tracker with us so that people could track our progress. One employee, an avid adventurist, woke his kids up to show them that we were reaching the summit. At the summit, we took out the Dovel sign for the picture. We had taken Dovel to new heights, and the Dovel team had traveled with us.[1]

Note

1 www.youtube.com/watch?v=7sQ6M7xqSmk&t=137s

16

CONCLUSION

Elma

Writing this book has been a wonderful trip down memory lane, as well as a full recognition of what we have accomplished together; also, writing a book together is yet another major project together, one we can write a book about. We had to decide on the objective and the mission of the book, as well as on the strategy: who was going to write about what (swim lanes) and what would be the overall style and format. While Dov has been advertising the upcoming book release to everyone and everywhere, I am more tentative and want to see the final product first. But just as we've always done, we respect each other's strengths and opinions; we recognize that neither of us holds the key to the truth on how to write a book, and we give each other space.

It is my deepest wish that this book has been valuable, useful, and entertaining to you, and that, at the end of it, you have a little more understanding and knowledge, and a lot more questions about what it takes to be "Partners in Life and Work".

DOI: 10.4324/9781003260653-19

Dov: When we decided to write this book, neither one of us knew exactly what we were getting into, but we believed that we could write a book that would have been helpful to us had we read it at any time during the history of Dovel. We also wanted to provide insight and lessons we learned through the years as we were hoping that this may help you as you are traveling on this road.

We know that every company and company founder(s) travels a unique path with a unique set of challenges and rewards. But, comparing our story to that of other start-ups, we also see commonalities.

As a technologist, this book took me down memory lane as I was thinking and writing about the tremendous changes that impacted the world over the past 35 years, and the changes that continue to accelerate. So where will we be in 20 to 30 years? Only time will tell, however, it is guaranteed to be a wild ride for many companies.

ABOUT THE AUTHORS

Figure A.1 Elma Levy

ELMA LEVY

Elma Levy is an entrepreneur, investor, leadership coach, and public speaker. Ms. Levy is cofounder and principal (with her husband, Dov) of the Eldov Group, LLC, a boutique investment and start-up advisory in the Washington, D.C., area. As an advisor to entrepreneurs, Ms. Levy provides advice on corporate governance, financial management, and tactical planning.

In 2000, Ms. Levy became the cofounder of Dovel Technologies, a company that builds and supports information technology (IT) systems for the federal government. Over the next 18 years, she served as chief executive officer and later as Chair of the Board, overseeing corporate governance and managing its infrastructure development and growth through its 2019 acquisition.

Ms. Levy is a credentialed leadership, wellness, and life skills coach and founder of Coach To Strength LLC in Bethesda, Maryland. Ms. Levy completed George Mason University's Leadership Coaching for Organizational Wellness program, Harvard Extension's Leadership Coaching Strategies program through its Division of Continuing Education, and the Life Skills Coaching program through the Life Coach Institute.

Ms. Levy is actively involved in Washington, D.C., and Maryland community business, academic, and nonprofit organizations. She is a member of the national advisory council for the George Washington University's School of Engineering (GW SEAS) and the advisory committee for the GWU SEAS Center for Women in Engineering. She is a business mentor, a professional development workshop presenter for the D.C. chapter of SCORE, and the Chair of the Board of directors (until May 2022) for Montgomery Hospice in Maryland.

Before becoming an entrepreneur and business owner, Ms. Levy was a family nurse practitioner. She practiced health care and case management in the U.S., Israel, and The Netherlands. Ms. Levy earned a BSN at George Mason University in Fairfax, Virginia, and an MSN and an FNP certification at Marymount University in Arlington, Virginia. In addition, in 2018, she completed the Women on Boards program at the Harvard Business School.

Ms. Levy and her husband, Dov, have two children, Mark and Karyn, and in 2020, they became first-time grandparents to Karyn's daughter, Isabelle Marie.

Born in the Netherlands, Ms. Levy relocated to Washington, D.C., in 1982 and is a U.S. citizen. Ms. Levy and her husband reside in Bethesda, Maryland, with their golden retriever named Rosie.

DOV LEVY

Figure A.2 Dov Levy

Dov Levy is an entrepreneur, investor, and a leading expert in large-scale mission-critical IT solutions.

Mr. Levy is the cofounder of Dovel Technologies, which he started with his wife, Elma Levy.

Mr. Levy has been the technical catalyst for Dovel Technologies' growth and innovation. He is a dynamic leader at the forefront of technological innovations.

Over the past three decades, Mr. Levy has served in technology leadership positions for the U.S. government's most significant mission-critical projects, such as the Electronic Data Gathering and Retrieval system for the U.S. Securities and Exchange Commission, the Defense Travel System for the Department of Defense, and GrantSolutions.gov.

Mr. Levy is cofounder and principal (with Elma) of the Eldov Group, LLC, a boutique investment and start-up advisory company. Mr. Levy is a senior advisor for GrantSolutions.gov, managing a large-scale implementation of cloud computing, event sourcing, machine learning, blockchain, and artificial intelligence.

In 2018, the George Washington University's School of Engineering and Applied Science (SEAS) inducted Elma and Dov Levy into the GW Engineering Hall of Fame for their sustained contributions as entrepreneurs, government consultants, and technology innovators.

Mr. Levy earned a bachelor's degree in geodetic science from Tel Aviv University and a master's degree in computer science from George Washington University.

INDEX

Note: Page numbers in *italics* indicate a figure and page numbers in **bold** indicate a table on the corresponding page.

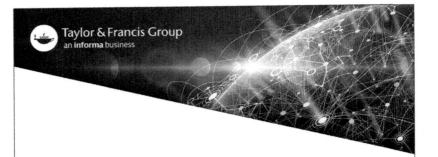